D

THE POET IN THE THEATRE

THE POET IN THE THEATRE

RONALD PEACOCK

A DRAMABOOK
HILL AND WANG—NEW YORK

Library of Congress Catalog Card Number: 60-13994
Manufactured in the United States of America

To

MY FATHER

MY FIRST GUIDE TO
BOOKS AND PLAYS

CONTENTS

PREFACE TO 1960 EDITION

When asked if I would agree to this book being reprinted my first impulse was to revise and extend it. But I quickly realized that this could not be done without changing its character so much that it would be simpler to write a completely new book. I have indeed acceded to a request and added the two essays on Goethe and Büchner, since it seems to me that they fit very well into the plan, which was to discuss problems of poetic form in later nineteenth- and twentieth-century drama. But if I had added essays on twentieth-century figures, on Cocteau, for example, or Claudel, both obviously "poets in the theatre," then why not also on Giraudoux, and Lorca, and Brecht, and Maxwell Anderson, and half a dozen others with an equal claim for consideration within the context of poetic drama? Such additions would have transformed the book into something more like a history or review of modern drama, a new book with a different point of view. So I have left it unaltered, except for the additions referred to, and it retains the character it had when it appeared.

It grew out of a mood of protest against the stock drama of social criticism that was the staple diet still offered to playgoers even in the later thirties; and it attempted to diagnose a situation of crisis in the drama by considering especially the work of writers who had in some way experienced acutely the conflict between poetic ideals and the predominant taste for realism and social problems. One reviewer, I remember, remarked that I was on the side of the angels. Well of course I was. The point was that angels on the whole no longer dwelt among men, and the few who were trying to were having a hard struggle to find a welcome. It is easily forgotten now that Eliot, Lorca, Cocteau, Giraudoux, and others, though already writing in the thirties, were only accepted wholeheartedly in the theatre after the war, in the late forties and the fifties.

One comment I should like to add. I am not the enemy of Ibsen that some critics, after reading the chapter on him in this book, have supposed. In naming it "Effects of Ibsen," and referring specifically to the theme of social criticism, I thought it would be clear that only one aspect of Ibsen was under consideration. I even went out of my way to say that the enormous influence of the "social" plays had prevented a greater knowledge and understanding of Ibsen's work as a whole. I think I was right about this. In the postwar period a number of excellent studies have appeared which correct previous one-sided views. Above all, the shift of interest toward the psychological and symbolic later plays is noteworthy, because it runs parallel to the success of new poetic styles in the postwar theatre. It is not too much to say that the growth of the poetic movement has itself liberated the greater Ibsen; the change in taste it brought has opened our eyes again to the poet Ibsen who had stood in the shadow of the critic of society.

Finally, in the preface to the first edition, I said that some comments on Cocteau's "poésie de théâtre" would have been especially appropriate, but at that time, in the war years, circumstances prevented me and most others from having any extensive acquaintance with his plays in the theatre, nor was his film work as widely known as it has since become. I should have added something now except that I have expressed my views on Cocteau in my later book, *The Art of Drama*, to which the interested reader is referred.

My thanks are due to the Editor of the *Publications of the English Goethe Society*, and to the Editors of *German Life and Letters*, for permission to reprint the essays on Goethe and Büchner, which originally appeared in those journals respectively.

R. P.

PREFACE

THE RELATIONS between poetry and theatre provide the theme of the following essays. They were not conceived as a historical account, but taken as a whole they do contain a story; the record of how a few authors tried to maintain the poetic integrity of drama against competition from outside and inside. Outside, there was novel and lyric, and in the period since 1870 or so, poetic life has flowed more easily in both these forms. Inside, there was the realistic drama in prose which generally had for subject a social or moral criticism of middle-class life. And of course there was the evil influence of commercialism in the theatre.

The study of this period, resembling at its gloomiest a post-mortem examination of a suspicious and very dead body, and discovering at its brightest more good things than might have been expected, raises many interesting questions. It directs the attention in fact to very deep ones, and forcibly. When an art form is under a cloud, and we begin to ask why, we are engaged before long in an inquiry into the form as well as its eclipse. The central question shapes itself as a complex one: What, in the nature of dramatic poetry, accounts for its scarcity in certain conditions? Why did poetry come to terms with the theatre only in occasional flashes, and with the greatest difficulty, and in unorthodox ways, in the period under review?

Each of my authors illustrates in a particularly striking manner some aspect of the main problem. The earliest in time, Grillparzer and Hebbel, writing between 1820 and

1860, are a link and a prelude. They belong to the last significant tradition of dramatic poetry in Europe, the last sustained effort of a succession of writers; but they forecast, in different ways, the major developments of the later nineteenth century. I have discussed Ibsen's influence rather than Ibsen as a whole, because it was his "social problem" plays that were so important for the character of much dramatic writing in Europe and occasioned the most powerful competition against poetry. The case of Shaw follows naturally and he is here presented to throw light on an aspect of the poetry-prose conflict arising from Ibsenism. With Chekhov and Synge another related problem emerges; the conception is wholly poetic, the medium prose, and in their time they both stand as encouraging reminders that a drama in prose can have an imaginative vitality that brings it very close to poetry. The inclusion of Henry James may give surprise. But he had a personal problem about drama and it merges in the general problem of drama in the literary situation of his time. Little attention has been paid to either, and I think only Stephen Spender has shown himself aware of deeper implications, without, however, going into them.

There is a connexion between James and Yeats, who had obviously to be in; it lies in their more subtle sense of mental experience, and the search for a technique of presenting it in the hostile conditions of the theatre. But Yeats is also very close to Hofmannsthal. They were contemporary and began under the predominant influence of French symbolist poetry, and in trying to find a form of poetry in the theatre, they both, in spite of very different subjects and outlook, show a certain similarity of approach and to some extent of technique. And they both lead to T. S. Eliot, whose work illumines retrospectively most of the problems of the whole period and shows an impressive attempt to stabilize a proper conception of what poetic values in the theatre are.

The knowledgeable reader will observe that no separate

essay is devoted to a French writer, though there have been a number of notable dramatists in France since 1850. None, however, would be a more pertinent or powerful illustration for my main theme than the writers I have chosen; and it was not in my scheme to write a survey of drama. But where the occasion demanded it, I have referred to French writers both of the last century and this. If I had singled out anyone for special treatment it would have been Cocteau, because his original use of myth and his conception of a *poésie du théâtre* certainly are relevant to my theme. But it would be peculiarly hazardous to talk about his work without having seen it in the theatre.

The essays are interconnected in many ways, and the links do not depend on any particular sequence. The arrangement here adopted has perhaps certain advantages; it may be found especially that taking Eliot and James first gives more quickly a comprehensive view of the whole situation, after which the place of the others in the pattern is more easily seen.

I should like to express my gratitude to Mr. Herbert Read for his advice and encouragement.

R. P.

THE POET IN THE THEATRE

T. S. ELIOT

ELIOT'S first great merit in respect of English drama is simply to have challenged a whole period by criticism and practice. The crux of the problem was the lack of poetry and style, and the degree of failure, the continued adherence to false ideals, made it necessary to search afresh for the foundations of the art. In "Rhetoric and Poetic Drama," "The Possibility of a Poetic Drama," "Dialogue on Dramatic Poetry," and essays on various dramatic poets, Eliot performed the task of restating with precision and authority some first principles. He was free from the sort of restriction that weighs on the professional critic, the daily debt to be paid to the world of theatrical entertainment and its public, and the integrity and assurance of his own work reinforced his detachment. But his two important dramas having in the meantime appeared, his effectiveness is seen now even more clearly than when he was writing his criticism. As examples to his precepts they clarify his creative aims, providing the idea of an alternative to the kind of drama against which his criticism was directed. What degree of dramatic genius Eliot possesses is of secondary interest in determining this first merit of his; the primary thing is that he has substantiated his views with adequate illustrations that can serve as touchstones.

There is a direct line of development from Eliot's criticism and earlier verse to *Murder in the Cathedral* and *The Family Reunion*. It might seem at first that the plays are an altogether new departure; but it is not so, nor do they spring from a mere academic interest in a form and its renewal. They are an extension of his verse. He himself has pointed out that much lyric verse is really dramatic in form; and it is his own inclinations that lead to the observation. His early orientation towards dramatic statement is, moreover, one aspect of his revolt against romantic lyricism. The significant early reaction against this poetic ideal is to be found, of course, in Browning's dramatic monologues, and a formal link is apparent between *Men and Women* and the characters of Eliot's poems. When Eliot asks "What great poetry is not dramatic?" he is to a large extent side-stepping romantic poetry and trying to pick up again an older tradition. It is worth noting that he draws near to a belief of Lessing—a pre-romantic writer—who maintained that dramatic poetry contains the sum of poetic achievement. After creating the "characters" of Sweeney and Prufrock and The Lady, it is but a step to Archbishop Becket and Harry Lord Monchensey. The former are emergent figures of drama; the latter are figures in the completed dramatic setting. At the same time the extreme degree to which they as single individuals contribute to the drama its real life is a reminder of the kind of dramatic poem from which they evolved.

A faulty understanding of this development is responsible for some hostile criticism of Eliot's verse dramas on grounds of conventionality. The main objection seems to be that their poetry has become less original and even retrograde. The verse is plainer, easier to follow, and less allusive; there is less tense short-circuiting, fewer images of startling novelty; and the whole poetic style being used to support a "reactionary" religious outlook, for which the critics have a distaste, it is held to have lost the vital freshness and significance of the poet's earlier work. But from the point of view of drama it is difficult to accept the notion of decline. On the contrary, Eliot's changed style would seem to be a proper development and adaptation of his verse for the conditions of the theatre. It is a simple logical step carrying his revolution a stage further.

In taking verse to drama again and drama to verse Eliot made a move of complex significance. It was at once a renovation of verse and a revival of drama. It was a breakaway from poetry conceived too exclusively as the expression of the sentient anarchic individual, and a return to the wider conception of it as a presentation of human actions with their reverberations in human society. And it was a restoration to drama of poetic conventions that intensify its "degree of form," to use Eliot's own term. The field of verse is widened again; the form of drama heightened.

For the assessment of Eliot's dramatic qualities one naturally turns to comparison with other dramatists. It is easy to see that he has not the sheer genius for drama that its characteristic masters, Shakespeare or Racine or Ibsen, have, and that some "born writers of the theatre" such as O'Neill possess, however prosaic their work. But his religious themes give his plays a character of their own. He reintegrates drama into a framework of ritual, and such an inspiration is so different from that of the dramatists named that the comparison loses some of its force. We are dealing with something that imposes conditions of its own and has to be judged accordingly.

Eliot's peculiar power resides in the way he depicts through the sensuous presence of persons the reality of the spirit and its religious experience. From this point of view a world of conflicting characters and complicated action such as that of Elizabethan drama becomes less appropriate as a main canon of judgement. There is sufficient character, in the sense of idiosyncrasy, to make the persons of Eliot's plays lifelike and actable. The nearest the poet comes to creating a character in the conventional sense is Amy, Harry's mother, in *The Family Reunion*, who dominates life at Wishwood with a tenacity of purpose that almost reaches ferocity. But in the case of the leading persons, Becket and Harry, their "characters" are nothing beside the presentation of their soul. They do not live independently, implementing their will, imposing their desires, fighting against other wills and desires; they are not opposed to other human beings in the drama of egoistic assertion that is universally and continually being enacted. They are agents of suffering in whom is made apparent the truth of particular religious conceptions. Their election to their destiny is the drama that Eliot presents, a drama that is at once intensely human and more than human, inhering in life and surpassing it in a divine plan. Nothing grips one so much in these plays as the compelling sense of spiritual powers that have a real operation above life and in it, transcending human experience but working through it; and the vividness of the communication is a mark of spiritual conviction and poetic imagination in the closest union. As a presentation of religious–Christian–experience in the dramatic form these plays are an outstanding achievement; for though it is often said that the drama in Europe originated in Christian festivals, it is rarely observed that at the higher levels it has been largely non-religious in its themes ever since. Those who deplore Eliot's later work as conventional might upon reconsideration find here a remarkable originality.

The ritual element in Eliot's plays emerges with particular clarity if one compares *Murder in the Cathedral* with Corneille's "Tragédie chrétienne" *Polyeucte,* one of the very few "Christian" dramas. Both portray the passion and death of a martyr. But Corneille makes of his subject-matter a tragic drama according to the established conventions. There are all the necessary elements of conflict, fears and jealousies and rivalries, there is a tangled action with a crisis of misunderstanding and a tragic issue. The play would not be by Corneille if it had not an undertone of lyrical enthusiasm for the greatness of soul and the fortitude displayed by early Christian martyrs. But it is certainly a play, a spectacle, presented for the esthetic delight of an audience, like *Le Cid* and *Horace*, and other works of the same author. It has nothing to do with ritual.

In *Murder in the Cathedral*, on the other hand, ritual belongs both to the inner structure of the play and to its performance. Through creating direct links at various points with his audience the poet has made his work into a continuous invitation to celebrate in religious fellowship the spiritual triumph of a saint. One link is provided by the obvious dovetailing of the sermon, and the apology of the Knights in the epilogue; another, more subtle one, by the priests, and the chorus composed of women of Canterbury. The spectacle of martyrdom is at the same time a celebration of spiritual triumph, the example of saintliness is an exhortation to Christian feeling. The drama becomes again an instrument of community.

The Family Reunion is not so obviously part and parcel of Christian worship as *Murder in the Cathedral.* But its ritualalistic character is not the less pronounced for being more ingenious and complex. The most remarkable feature is the interweaving of pagan rite and Christian meaning in a modern atmosphere of country house, racing-cars, Heads of Women's Colleges, steamships and ungrammatical chauffeurs.

Eliot has always obtained poetic effects by mingling seemingly incongruous things, and here the method is dramatically as well as poetically vivid. It goes deeper than technical device, for the interfusion comes with a natural truth from a mind accustomed to thinking in terms of the whole history of the human race, and from a sensibility that has expanded its range in contact with the most diverse kinds of expression from all periods of poetic activity. The linking of a ritual of primitive fear with a twentieth-century drawing-room by means of the arch of Christianity is an audacious piece of dramatic architecture, simplifying vision, concentrating emotion, throwing into vivid relief the vast dimensions of the spiritual drama involved. The problems this play treats in a Christian spirit are in themselves primeval and universal. It is a question of evil and its expurgation, the evil that is there from the beginning, the general guilt of man, prevalent at all times and in all races, of whatever religion. The drama of "sin and expiation" that Eliot presents is a Christian form of the universal tragedy. And I think its main effect is to express the tragic implications of life in their most generalized form. It is true, of course, that *King Lear* or *Macbeth* or *Othello* reflect the general evil; yet each remains a particular tragedy, the tragedy of Lear, of Macbeth, of Othello. Harry, the protagonist of *The Family Reunion*, is not comparable to them. He is used for a purpose more important than himself, to focus a transcendental reality and reflect a design of the spiritual world. Through him is presented the universal sin and agony. There is something comparable in *Murder in the Cathedral*, which adumbrates the tragic implications of Becket's martyrdom for the history of the Church. What happened through and after Becket's death: the triumph of the secular forces, the divorce of religion and the law of God from the temporal government of society, this is the tragedy that is consequent upon the happenings of the play.

It is quite possible that this generalization of evil and guilt is the only form in which tragic expression can be achieved in the present age, which is one of social disintegration. The individual is overshadowed by the conflict of impersonal forces, of which he is more and more the victim and less and less even so much as the agent. Moreover, the moral judgements of the time bear upon the non-personal, the social situation; the question of the rightness or wrongness, the luck or ill-luck, of individual behavior is disregarded and is often impossible of determination. A private crisis has little significance for a public eye dazzled by revolution and international vicissitudes. The "tragic hero" has in consequence disappeared. The tragic plays of O'Casey are symptomatic of this situation. His characters, vivid as some of them are, are not as important as the larger political tragedy of which they are fortuitous victims. In themselves they are not in the least inevitable and unique tragic persons, like those of tradition; any set of Dublin people would do. An earlier play like Chekhov's *Three Sisters* shows something similar (Chekhov is full of anticipations). There is in it no clear personal tragedy, but there is certainly a tragic "Stimmung" that derives from a social background, from the feeling for a general situation in which the personal becomes helpless and un-personal.

At the same time Eliot is distinguished from these writers by his marked retention of the central personage as the pivot of the whole drama. He has combined what might seem to be irreconcilable: the sense of impersonal tragedy in which all are involved, and the dominating interest of a personal destiny. This feat is not the less astonishing because it rests on the quite simple foundation of the Christian faith, with its doctrine of original sin and of the importance of the individual soul, the individual conscience. We are never told that Harry was guilty of the evil *act*, that he really did "push her over." We are given to understand that he was guilty of the evil *desire*, as his father and Agatha were before him; that was the knot to be unknotted, the cross to be uncrossed. Harry, as an individual, is necessary, because there must be expiation; but he expiates for many. In this interpretation the individual and the human race are inextricably intertwined, and that is what we see reflected in the remarkable feature we have observed. Here we discover the play's profoundest character, which is that of a passion drama. It is the subtlest development and completion of the religious and dramatic idea presented in *Murder in the Cathedral.* It bears a curious resemblance to Greek tragedy in its early evolution: the spectacle of the tragic hero who is really the impersonation of the sacrificed god Dionysus.

The great strength of Eliot's two plays being in their presentation of a spiritual conflict, it is their leading characters that are the most convincing dramatically. The tension is all in their struggle with themselves; other characters have less a part in this tension than in suspense, the suspense of simply waiting to see what happens to Becket and Harry. In consequence the drama runs in a narrow channel, but it runs with force and depth. The restoration of the verse convention has the greatest share in this success, for it allows the poet to unfold the life of the spirit, and he recovers for drama inwardness and detail in psychological portraiture.

In the situation of drama in our century this is extremely interesting. Psychology was one of the great new studies, and whilst it gave a powerful impetus to the novel, drama failed to exploit it (Strindbergian essays in abnormality can be left aside). A superficial view might be that psychological delineation fell more naturally within the scope of narrative. But Shakespeare and Racine are full of "psychology"; and Grillparzer, in a framework derived from Shakespeare, succeeds astonishingly in externalizing in stage incident what is going on inside the minds of his characters.

But unfortunately the new psychological interest came at a time when drama had got more and more fixed in the technique of "realism"; and that certainly is inimical to broad and detailed psychological delineation. Hence the interest that gave such an impetus to the novel is frustrated in the drama. The comparison is illuminating; for in the former, psychological breadth was itself an expansion of the "realistic" picture. But the novel did not make this gain by abandoning conventions; it created new ones to suit its new aim. Henry James is full of them. The structure of the language in which Joyce presents the "stream of consciousness" is also a convention. In this the novel showed itself aware of the necessity of conventions in all art; of those preliminary mechanisms that alone make possible an imaginative creation. Realist drama, on the other hand, aimed at dispensing with as many conventions as possible, which was to forgo too much. Verse, monologues, asides, long speeches savoured of "unreality" and were cast off. The substance of the human person, the very foundation of dramatic vitality, was whittled away, as this art found its pride in evading the very conditions in which it flourished best.

Ibsen's retrospective technique is, I think, a symptom of the difficulty facing drama at that time. It has all the appearance of being an attempt to meet simultaneously the contemporary demands of naturalism and the new ones of a fuller psychology. For the deep perspective of the past that he evokes by conversational reference is all a contribution to a psychological present. The method is remarkable in Ibsen's hands; less so with others who have tried it. It is not only that it is exacting; all art is exacting. It is too rigid and cramping.

A further symptom that the problem existed, and another attempt to solve it, was provided by O'Neill's *Strange Interlude;* it is grotesque and unworkable. And is it going too far to see still another symptom in some of Bernard's work, of which *Le Printemps des Autres* is an example? He can present a psychological crisis within a realist framework, but it is never actually *uttered;* it is suggested by a system of references and hints dropped in quiet, almost unobtrusive daily conversation and by those famous silences which made his work a centre of controversy. How great must the embarrassment of drama be, when so distinguished a writer is found skirting danger so closely. Silences have their expressiveness, but what great drama yet made silence its main point? Bernard is saved, because, like many French artists, he is particularly good at the exquisite suggestion, at subtle and delicate indirectness. The quality of his work shows what can be done, if it is necessary, without the support of the conventions we are speaking of. One can, however, admit different kinds of achievement in play-writing without forgetting the conditions in which drama is at its finest and richest. A glance back at classical work shows that Bernard is doing an extremely good job in circumstances that make for the contraction rather than the expansion of the art. Eliot's work shows, on the other hand, a recovery of the sense of possibilities; it brings a large breath of air from the great traditions of drama.

Another aspect of intellectual life in this century showed itself unfavourable to dramatic art: the sense of history, the voracious extension of all historical knowledge regarding human civilization, primitive and advanced, the awareness of time's accumulations, of the past in the present. Eliot and Joyce are the two authors who have shown themselves most sensitive to these developments, most deliberately conscious of their importance, and most concerned that imaginative writing should adjust itself to them. Their writing is saturated with the historical and literary culture of Europe, it is allusive in the extreme, it postulates a similar culture in the reader. The verse of the one, and the prose of the other, thus reacted quickly to the new intellectual climate. There is no drama that shows a similar reaction. The reason is obvious, for it is difficult to imagine a drama that would correspond to these two examples of modern writing and still be possible on the stage. The new development was essentially inimical to the acted drama. But the interesting thing is that both these writers, Eliot in lyric (before he wrote plays), Joyce in narrative, make an approach to drama, and in Eliot's case it is of the most deliberate kind. Of the latter we have already said something; with Joyce it is not difficult to see that the approach consists in the evasion of "reporting" and straight description, in the direct presentation of the complex of thoughts, ideas, emotions. This remarkable phenomenon is an acknowledgment of the peculiar power of dramatic statement; and that has historical and esthetic importance. In the midst of circumstances that are hostile to it, the dramatic form asserts itself under the cover of other forms. These two writers, having something to say that was unsuited to stage performance, use non-dramatic forms in such a way as to borrow the force of drama. They are thus linked, in the history of formal literary developments, with Henry James. He tried to compromise with the theatre, quarrelled with it, and withdrew. He then tried to find a "dramatic" form outside the theatre, by adapting the technique of the novel. He did it mainly by means of psychological focusing with scenic arrangements; and seen in perspective Joyce's work is the extreme logical outcome of the process. Eliot and Joyce, like James a generation earlier, pay their tribute to dramatic form even when they cannot use it in its theatre mode.

Later Eliot turns to the stage play; he does so after a great change has taken place not so much in his thought as in the relation between his thought and his poetic expression. The presentation of characters such as Prufrock, Gerontion and The Hollow Men may tend towards a dramatized version of lyric, but these characters in themselves are not positive enough to be the centres of a drama. They are negative, sterile, without energy. They are portrayed as representatives of unspiritual civilization and beliefless life. The whole presentation remains *semi*-dramatic because it cannot be more. Eliot's one attempt at strict drama from this earlier period, *Sweeney Agonistes*, remained a fragment. It has the interest of a technical experiment, but it would be wrong to attribute its incompletion to pure technical insufficiency. For Eliot uses a quotation from the *Choephoroi* to introduce it:

> ORESTES. You don't see them—but *I* see them: they are hunting me down, I must move on.

which shows that he was occupied already with the theme of *The Family Reunion*. At that stage, however, he had not found the right relation between theme, subject and form that was required to cast a complete drama.

This stage is reached after *Ash Wednesday*. Becket and Harry contrast with the earlier "characters" because they are positive personalities; positive in the sense that they have found a *reality* in suffering and religious experience. They incorporate the spiritual challenge that is only latent in the earlier poems; that one feels in *The Waste Land* is inevitable, but only to be sensed as yet in the shadows behind the poem.

An obvious poetic link between the plays and the earlier verse is in the choruses, especially those of *The Family Reunion*. Ivy, Gerald, Charles and Violet take up the old themes of emptiness and futility, irreligion and spiritual degradation, that we find in the Prufrock and Sweeney poems. Not only has the changed relationship between Eliot's thought and his poetry made drama possible for him; he has found a way of presenting the total picture, the positive and the negative together, the criticism and the challenge, the diagnosis and the spiritual remedy. The earlier work, hovering formally on the threshold of drama, shows an individual's sensitiveness to a spiritual situation. The struggle with that situation, the vision of good contending with the evil, finds a natural expression in the pure dramatic form.

In this development towards drama, Eliot has sacrificed the complex and obscure allusiveness of his earlier verse, the element of historical and literary reference which we have said was unsuited to drama. But the *sense* from which it sprang has by no means been sacrificed. It has found a subtle —and moreover an essentially dramatic—expression in *The Family Reunion* in the feature we discussed above: the use of a ritual that is an echo of primitive and pagan rites.

The construction of Eliot's two plays is simple and recalls in its general effect Greek and French "classical" models. Eliot admires the Three Unities, and though he has not followed them slavishly his deviation is not so great as to make him inconsistent with his declared admiration. The technique of revealing gradually past history in *The Family Reunion* owes also something to the method familiar in Ibsen. More important, however, than a mechanical observance of a particular sort of plan, or minor weaknesses of construction here and there, is the motive of his scheme; to keep the central character continuously in the centre. Harry and the Archbishop are both uninterruptedly present, either physically or spiritually. When they are on the scene, the other characters fall into a certain formal pattern of relationship to them. In *Murder in the Cathedral* the pattern is perhaps a little stiffly geometrical in the case of the Tempters and the Knights; in *The Family Reunion* it is more freely organized, but the sense of it is never lost. The cross-relationships between Harry and Amy and Agatha and Mary are such that even when Harry is not present, it is Harry's drama that continues to be played out by the others; for the drama of *their* lives only comes to its focus in Harry's fate. One of the delicate beauties of this play is the progressive illumination of the human pattern in its relationship to the spiritual pattern, until the unity of the whole is completely defined.

The Family Reunion is in this respect much superior to *Murder in the Cathedral*. In the latter the effect is rather of oversimplification than of the "simplicity" that is an ideal of design and at which Eliot aims. The way, for instance, the whole of the temporal external historical circumstances are compressed into the speeches of Tempters and Knights is a weakness; because the simplification is achieved too much at the expense of sensuous impact. The mere reference is not vivid enough; more might legitimately have been depicted. *The Family Reunion* achieves a better architectural style because its simplicity more nearly approaches that of the Greeks: it is the predominant sense of unity derived not from the absence but from the mastery of complexity, the restraint laid upon variety.

The use of a chorus is a further feature of an effort towards classical style. (Eliot uses the word unambiguously of his taste in poetry and we use it in the same sense.) The first function of the chorus in these two plays must be taken to be part of the general plan of stylization. From this point of view it has always been tempting for modern writers to imitate the Greeks; though the "classical" drama of France was conducted without this external prop. Modern experiments with a chorus are on the whole embarrassing, because they are artificial; there are no longer organic grounds, as there were in Greek drama, for the fusion of music, words and dance. Eliot's chorus in *Murder in the Cathedral* is imitative, fulfilling the intermediary function of the Greek chorus between the fable and the spectators, the myth and the believers. The chorus of *The Family Reunion*—we repeatedly notice its greater refinement—shows a much more intricate evolution. It is composed of four members of the family who are in the first instance an integral part of the general action and only at certain moments become a "chorus." Such moments are projections of the unheard and unspoken life that flows through the silences of the family reunion. Amy has gathered her relatives together at Wishwood and told them that Harry is returning and how they are to behave:

CHORUS (IVY, VIOLET, GERALD and CHARLES).
Why do we feel embarrassed, impatient, fretful, ill at ease,
Assembled like amateur actors who have not been assigned their parts?
Like amateur actors in a dream when the curtain rises, to find themselves dressed for a different play, or having rehearsed the wrong parts,
Waiting for the rustling in the stalls, the titter in the dress circle, the laughter and catcalls in the gallery?

CHARLES. I might have been in St. James's Street, in a comfortable chair rather nearer the fire.

IVY. I might have been visiting Cousin Lily at Sidmouth, if I had not had to come to this party.

GERALD. I might have been staying with Compton-Smith, down at his place in Dorset.

VIOLET. I should have been helping Lady Bumpus, at the Vicar's American Tea.

CHORUS. Yet we are here at Amy's command, to play an unread part in some monstrous farce, ridiculous in some nightmare pantomime.

Such a use of the chorus amounts to a new form of the aside, a formalized extension of it; and whilst it breaks away from realistic drama, it keeps the character of the setting. It is thus a use of the chorus that we are not accustomed to from the Greek, a use Eliot has invented. It is a very original treatment of a feature of drama that without a doubt has high formal value: and success is achieved without having to pay for it with artificiality. It is certainly a convention but an unobtrusive appropriate one, that weaves in and out of the substance of the play. It maintains, however, in a way the more vital and forceful for being indirect, the generalizing function of the Greek chorus, the direction of the common thought upon the events being witnessed.

In the matter of dramatic speech more light is thrown by Eliot himself on his aims than can come from a commentator. In general we observe the same natural expansion of an early tendency as we do in regard to the dramatic form in its larger constructive aspects. To derive poetic speech from living speech, poetic vocabulary from the vocabulary of modern life; to seek the precise word and image for true pictures and feelings, avoiding the romantic, conventional, the spurious, the used-up coinage of poetic phrase—this has always been an aim of Eliot. From this point of view again, therefore, we see how his drama is a continuing prosecution of a single revolutionary aim, to clear away the dead forms and create new ones. The dead forms here were blank verse and an emotionally false ideal of dignified dramatic idiom. It remains to suggest briefly, since a detailed analysis is beyond the scope of this essay, whether he has achieved his aims and where he has done so best.

There is one point of interest which might be considered first, however. Eliot has insisted so much on the way the Elizabethans evolved their form of dramatic verse from contemporary speech, and has made that so much the central technical problem, that a too simple parallel might be drawn between himself and them. For he is faced by a problem peculiar to the contemporary situation. He has to re-establish dramatic poetry against a multifarious hostility, including that of other forms of art and entertainment. For the Elizabethans the verse-drama was the predominant form of their age, with many forces working to maintain it. The novel holds that position today in literature; drama has to compete with it, and in addition with the film.

The domination of the novel has been linked so far with the prosperity and influence of the middle-class, to which Eliot belongs. As an observer and portrayer of life he has to face the fact that the social class he knows best has found its most vivid and complete expression in the novel from the eighteenth century onwards when it first consolidated political power; as medieval chivalrous society was presented in the romances, and Renaissance Kingship, princedom and individualism were expressed in the drama. When in 1735 Lillo wrote his play *George Barnwell* in an attempt to present tragedy in terms of the middle-class, he had certainly sensed the direction things were taking, and his step was historic. But the seed he scattered came to no growth. It was the novel that grew and flourished, whilst the drama collapsed. The development is common to all Europe, except Germany, where Lessing initiated a powerful tradition of dramatic poetry which was continued by Schiller and others, and for which I have suggested special reasons in another essay. Tributes were paid to the former grandeur of drama in the shape of literary artificialities or romantic extravagances: Sheridan Knowles in England, Victor Hugo in France. But in trying to fill the gap they only sharpen our sense of its size.

Drama with the middle-class as its setting only recovers some creative power when that class is beginning to disintegrate and calls for criticism rather than glorification. Dumas fils, treating problems of love and marriage, is the herald of the movement. Then comes Ibsen's weightier attack on the foundations of bourgeois society, then the whole social problem drama in Ibsen's wake. Drama revives, therefore, but owes too much to a critical impulse, too little to imaginative creation.

The foundation for Eliot's new dramatic poetry is a spiritual theme that transcends the bourgeois or any other particular class milieu. However rooted in the middle-class he is, socially speaking, he seems to have realized, consciously or unconsciously, the implications for drama and poetry of the facts of dramatic history we have just touched upon. In *Murder in the Cathedral* the poet is helped very greatly by the *historical* character of the subject, apart from its spiritual theme. It was a fortunate and judicious choice for a revival of poetic drama, since the poetic treatment derives support from the great body of historical drama in verse. In *The Family Reunion* Eliot has confronted the bolder task and the severer test in making the action of the play contemporary. A subtle ambiguity gives him his solution. His people live the life and talk the language of the modern upper middle-class; they are, however, technically aristocratic. In this there is a suggestion of classlessness, in spite of the marked character of the milieu; and the ambiguity is emphasized by the exclusive use of Christian names. These people are, moreover, like those of Henry James, largely independent of mere harrowing labour, and in consequence their inner life unfolds itself the more richly, or the emptiness of their lives is the more striking and appalling, giving the poet the contrast he is intent on. Eliot, therefore, portrays in this way the class best known to his observation, and also the one that he can lift most suitably and divest of its merely social character into the poetry of his spiritual theme.

As a result, it is this play that gives the poet his greatest opportunities for stylizing the natural language of present-day conversation, and his greatest successes. His handling of intimate family talk, his overlaying of everyday speech with delicate tones of poetry, is here at its most felicitous. The speeches of the Knights in *Murder in the Cathedral* are perhaps a preliminary form of these developments. Those of the Tempters still show not so much naturalness as the kind of syntactic clipping that has been much experimented with in recent verse in the attempt to achieve a new crispness and liveliness:

> King in England is not all-powerful;
> King is in France, squabbling in Anjou;
> Round him waiting hungry sons.

or:

> You know truly, the King will never trust
> Twice, the man who has been his friend.
> Borrow use cautiously, employ
> Your services as long as you have to lend.
> You would wait for trap to snap
> Having served your turn, broken and crushed.
> As for barons, envy of lesser men
> Is still more stubborn than king's anger.

Or there are flights into a speech in which the degree of poetic effort is sensibly greater:

> Your thoughts have more power than kings to compel you.
> You have also thought, sometimes at your prayers,
> Sometimes hesitating at the angles of stairs,
> And between sleep and waking, early in the morning,
> When the bird cries, have thought of further scorning.

That nothing lasts, but the wheel turns,
The nest is rifled, and the bird mourns;
That the shrine shall be pillaged, and the gold spent,
The jewels gone for the light ladies' ornament,
The sanctuary broken, and its stores
Swept into the laps of parasites and whores.
When miracles cease, and the faithful desert you,
And men shall only do their best to forget you.
And later is worse, when men will not hate you
Enough to defame or to execrate you,
But pondering the qualities that you lacked
Will only try to find the historical fact.
When men shall declare that there was no mystery
About this man who played a certain part in history.

The idiom of this passage is quite appropriate in this play, but it is already detached from a specifically "modern" setting. It is something quite different from the particular achievement of which we are speaking in relation to *The Family Reunion.* Here is a passage from the latter play:

VIOLET. Well, Harry,
I think that you might have something to say.
Aren't you sorry for your brother? Aren't you aware
Of what is going on? and what it means to your mother?
HARRY. Oh, of course I'm sorry. But from what Winchell says
I don't think the matter can be very serious.
A minor trouble like a concussion
Cannot make very much difference to John.
A brief vacation from the kind of consciousness
That John enjoys, can't make very much difference
To him or to anyone else. If he was ever really conscious
I should be glad for him to have a breathing spell:
But John's ordinary day isn't much more than breathing.
IVY. Really, Harry! how can you be so callous?
I always thought you were so fond of John.
VIOLET. And if you don't care what happens to John,
You might show some consideration to your mother.
AMY. I do not know very much:
And as I get older, I am coming to think
How little I have ever known.

But I think your remarks are much more inappropriate
Than Harry's.
HARRY. It's only when they see nothing
That people can always show the suitable emotions—
And so far as they feel at all, their emotions are suitable.
They don't understand what it is to be awake,
To be living on several planes at once
Though one cannot speak with several voices at once.
I have all of the rightminded feeling about John
That you consider appropriate. Only, that's not the language
That I choose to be talking. I will not talk yours.
AMY. You looked like your father
When you said that.
HARRY. I think, mother,
I shall make you lie down. You must be very tired.

This illustrates very well, I think, how closely the poet is working to the present-day spoken idiom. His unrigid rhythms give to the easiest conversational phrasing a stylization that is sufficient to preserve the unity of tone, whilst the thought and feeling can pass at any moment with subtlety and facility to a greater intensity, as for example in Harry's speech beginning "It's only when they see nothing" or again, a little later, in the significant speech:

Mother is asleep, I think: it's strange how the old
Can drop off to sleep in the middle of calamity
Like children, or like hardened campaigners.

There are many "finer" passages, but the poetry of those quoted being more subdued they illustrate better the point under discussion.

How remarkable a sense of the problem Eliot has and how fine a taste he has shown in handling it is apparent in another way. For the attempted solution to succeed, the modern vocabulary and the world of things it represents needed a particularly *musical* transfiguration:

We all of us make the pretension
To be the uncommon exception

To the universal bondage.
We like to appear in the newspapers
So long as we are in the right column.
We know about the railway accident
We know about the sudden thrombosis
And the slowly hardening artery,
We like to be thought well of by others
So that we may think well of ourselves.
And any explanation will satisfy:
We only ask to be reassured
About the noises in the cellar
And the window that should not have been open.

Or:

We understand the ordinary business of living,
We know how to work the machine,
We can usually avoid accidents,
We are insured against fire,
Against larceny and illness,
Against defective plumbing,
But not against the act of God.
We know various spells and enchantments,
And minor forms of sorcery,
Divination and chiromancy,
Specifics against insomnia,
Lumbago, and the loss of money.
But the circle of our understanding
Is a very restricted area.
Except for a limited number
Of strictly practical purposes
We do not know what we are doing;
And even, when you think of it,
We do not know much about thinking.
What is happening outside of the circle?
And what is the meaning of happening?
What ambush lies beyond the heather
And behind the Standing Stones?
Beyond the Heaviside Layer
And behind the smiling moon?
And what is being done to us?
And what are we, and what are we doing?

To each and all of these questions
There is no conceivable answer.
We have suffered far more than a personal loss—
We have lost our way in the dark.

It is a unique achievement to have produced this new music of dramatic language. Lines with a clear rhythmic accent but definite syllable value give the poet a great part of his effect through their suppleness and variety of cadence. But the rhythm of words is not independent of their meaning, and the musical effect is greatest where spiritual temper is detached forcefully but without strain amidst the characteristic symbols and thoughts of a modern environment. And it is perhaps especially remarkable that he achieves this with a language that is consistently precise and lucid. The emotional suggestiveness, the undertones and overtones that have always made romantic lyric appear closer to music than any other are here spurned.

Even if Eliot writes no more plays, there is sufficient in *Murder in the Cathedral* and *The Family Reunion* to make them important of themselves, and certainly an integral part of his poetry as a whole. Beyond that, however, they have a significance quite disproportionate to their bulk in connection with the situation of drama in Eliot's generation, and now. The later play, however it may be judged in the future by a changing taste, remains extraordinary in this twofold way. So many problems of Eliot's own personal development, and so many problems of the drama of the present age in relation to poetry, find here their resolution. One feels perhaps a certain amount of strain; Eliot's dramatic genius does not flow abundantly. But he has to do spade-work. We have only to look at the Irish drama to see how many swimmers weak and strong the current of a tradition, once created, will carry. Eliot had not this advantage. On the other hand, an extreme degree of critical introspection such as he possesses, and the sensitive and precise awareness of a literary *situation* as distinct from his own personal urges, were an advantage for his purpose. His drama shows that he has not only made a major contribution towards reshaping the language of poetry in its narrower lyric aspect, but towards a new extension of modern poetry by an extension of the world it portrays. As a poet facing the challenge of the novel, with all the theories of the day that support the novel not only as "the form" of today but of tomorrow also, he has done something to recover the breadth of poetry, making it again an interpretation of human action as well as of individual dream.

HENRY JAMES AND THE DRAMA

NO ONE is very curious about the plays of Henry James, even in this present day of his glory; yet he is an interesting figure for the history of drama in the last fifty years. Amongst English writers he is one of those—a minority—who have an exceptionally refined sense of formal values. The word "pattern" has become a commonplace echo to his name. He admired the French with their faculty of design. He had a predilection for the concentration of the nouvellé, a form much stricter than the novel. In a period of drama characterized above all by low ideals of form, by the absence of style, it was at least a moment fraught with possibilities when so pronounced an artist turned to it, doing so, moreover, with an intense feeling that this was "his form," as Henry James did about the year 1890. What a prospect of delicate art, perhaps above all of a wise and gracious comedy, opened up for the theatre through James's interest. The theatrical career upon which he launched himself with tenacity and hope came, however, to a disastrous end. But his failure is of the kind that are as instructive as successes. It throws light on a number of questions connected with literary inspiration and form; on his own genius; on the drama in relation to the novel; on the plight of modern drama in England.

What attracted James to play-writing? In the letters written during the years in which he wrestled with the theatre he insists very much on the necessity of making money, for his books were bringing him none; and one might think, to read him, that it really was his principal concern. But his frank profession of profit-seeking is as little convincing as more customary professions of disinterestedness. There are many signs that the demon of the theatre could take possession of James without regard to finance. In a letter to Elizabeth Robins, for instance (7 Dec. 1893), he refers to the fact that he is "incurable in that perverse tendency" (i.e. to the stage) and that he will live, probably, "to be as much disconcerted and deluded yet again." A more explicit passage to William James reveals the full measure of his artistic seriousness and also the doubts to be overcome, the little *arrière-pensées*, the reservations that prevented him from letting himself go completely. "Now that I have tasted blood, c'est une rage (of determination to *do*, and triumph, on my part) for I feel at last as if I had found my *real* form, which I am capable of carrying far, and for which the pale little art of fiction, as I have practised it, has been, for me, but a limited and restricted substitute. The strange thing is that I always, universally, knew *this* was my more characteristic form—but was kept away from it by a half-modest, half-exaggerated sense of the difficulty (that is, I mean the practical odiousness) of the conditions. But now that I have accepted them and met them, I see that one isn't at all, needfully, their victim, but is, from the moment one *is* anything, one's self, worth speaking of, their *master;* and may use them, command them, squeeze them, lift them up and better them. As for the form *itself*, its honour and inspiration are (à défaut d'autres) in its difficulty. If it were easy to write a good play I couldn't and wouldn't think of it; but it is in fact damnably hard (to this truth the paucity of the article—in the English-speaking world—testifies), and that constitutes a solid respectability—guarantees one's intellectual self-respect" (6 Feb. 1891). He repeats the idea to R. L. Stevenson: "All the same, I feel as if I had at last *found* my form—my real one—that for which pale fiction is an ineffectual substitute" (18 Feb. 1891); and he adds, confident and indeed quite remarkably undaunted by the "difficulty" he stresses: "God grant this unholy truth may not abide with me more than two or three years—time to dig out eight or ten rounded masterpieces. . . ." Admitting a tinge of irony in the use of "masterpieces," the moment in which James saw for himself such a traffic in successful plays can be described as a buoyant one; it confirms, however, the *élan* of his preoccupation.

In his approach to the problem James found two major difficulties: the acquisition of what was for him as a novelist an entirely new technique; and the choice of subject. "I do think," he wrote to Miss Robins, "the kinds of subject for novel and play essentially differ." He directed his effort first against the technical difficulty, and technique he conceived in the largest terms: the planning and composing of an action under due consideration of all the circumstances of the theatre, such as the availability of actors and actresses, their habits, temperaments, vanities; the theatres to be used, its manager and properties; the audience, its whims and predilections and limitations. James went into it, he thought it out. "The convenience the piece had to square with," he says of *The Reprobate*, "was the idea of a short comedy, the broader the better, thoroughly simple, intensely 'pleasant,' affording a liberal chance to a young sympathetic comedian, calling for as little acting as possible besides, skirting the fairy-tale, straining any and every point for that agreeable falsity, entailing no expense in mounting, and supremely susceptible of being played to audiences unaccustomed to beat about the bush for their amusement—audiences, to be perfectly honest, in country towns. This last condition was rigorous for both pieces, and the one the author took most into account."

The result of taking so many pains was a batch of comedies that remain rather conventional in spite of much ingenuity and promise. The four that are available to the reader now, printed as *Theatricals*, first and second series, give a fair idea of how James conceived the problem. A brief indication of their plots will be useful.

In *Tenants* Sir Frederick Byng has a son Norman and a ward Mildred, who fall in love with each other. Sir Frederick wishes to avoid the appearance of wanting the considerable fortune of his ward for his son, and so he sends him off to India. A former mistress of his, Mrs. Vibert, arrives on the scene with their illegitimate son Claude, and a Captain Lurcher. The latter is the accomplice in Mrs. Vibert's plot to warm up Sir Frederick's old love for her and thus through him find a way of catching the ward and her money for Claude. Mildred sees through their scheme and cables at once to Norman to return. He arrives in time to save the situation. The unfortunate Claude discovers his position, which he hadn't known, and the Viberts leave.

The action of *Disengaged* takes place in a disagreeable atmosphere of flirtation, in which a Captain Prime finds himself forced by a practical joke into a compromising situation with a most unattractive girl, from which he cannot with honour escape; he must offer her marriage. Mrs. Jaspers, a beautiful young widow whom all the men run after, discovers that she loves the Captain, and by the exercise of ingenuity and moral blandishments gets him out of his predicament.

The Reprobate develops the idea that a man who is supposed to be wicked and is kept closely confined does not in consequence himself know whether he is vicious or not. When temptations are put in his way by a sympathetic friend he discovers he is immune to them. So with the help of the same friend, and a girl he loves, he breaks out and turns the tables on his oppressors.

The plot of *The Album* turns on procuring a fortune for the rightful heir. Mark Bernal, long given up for lost or dead, happens to turn up at the moment when his cousin Bedford is dying. But Sir Ralph Damant, next of kin after Bernal, is in the house, and although he hears of a new arrival and sees an album of sketches with the name Mark Bernal on them, he withholds the knowledge from the dying man and his lawyers and thus procures the fortune for himself. He has, however, aroused the suspicions of Grace Jesmond, Bedford's secretary. She wishes the rightful heir–Bernal–to have justice done to him; and her natural scruples about justice are fortified by an awakening love for Bernal, which, however, she conceals. The intrigue depends on her fight against Sir Ralph Damant's gross materialism, and the suspicions cast on her by other persons involved to the effect that *she* wants the money of her former employer.

These mere outlines may suffice to show James's generosity in the matter of meeting the "demands" of the theatre and its public. The types he uses belong to the standard material of entertainment drama: villains, hypocrites, masterful women, flirts, fond mothers and stupid daughters, philanderers, many intriguers for money and marriage, ideal heroes and heroines. There is a good deal of melodramatic colour. The hero or heroine do not at first shine with all their virtue. They appear rather as bad lots or at least as persons of dubious motive. But in the end they turn out beautifully to be the very best sort of genuine good characters, whilst the selfish, materialistic, and wicked people are put morally in their places.

One recognizes the great artist we know in the "surface" of these plays, in their ingenuity, in their delicacy of touch, in their beautifully modulated dialogue, which is crisp, clear, and graceful. They bear the promise of a *style* quite out of proportion to their makeshift subject-matter, and unique in the play-writing of the day. Here is an excerpt from the first act of *The Album:*

BERNAL. . . . Where's Miss Jesmond?
SIR RALPH. She has left me, thank God!
BERNAL (*surprised*). Why abnormal gratitude?
SIR RALPH. For miraculous relief. She wants to marry me. She is like the others.

B. The others?

S. R. The old woman and the girl. They've marked me, you know. But Miss Jesmond has marked me biggest.

B. (*amused*). In bright red chalk?

S. R. (*with a nervous wriggle*). I feel it between the shoulders! She's an *intrigante*—of a peculiarly dangerous type.

B. Why, I thought her so charming!

S. R. She has made up to you too?

B. (*smiling*). Like the others!

S. R. She's a hungry adventuress.

B. With me it doesn't matter; I'm not worth their powder.

S. R. Because you're poor?

B. Because I'm nobody.

S. R. Be duly grateful. It protects you.

B. My dear man, I like danger!

S. R. You don't know it! To know it, you must be exposed.

B. I see—even as you are.

S. R. My position is one of the highest peril.

B. You're a match, a catch, a swell: you pay for it!

S. R. I pay too much and too often. I pay with my comfort, my health, my nerves! My nerves are gone to pieces—I live in a state of siege!

B. But you seem to hold out.

S. R. There are very serious breaches. It's the modern methods of attack—they've reduced it to a science.

B. Lady Basset's a kind of Moltke?

S. R. And Miss Jesmond's a kind of Armstrong! I vow I'm doomed to fall!

B. My dear fellow, don't you desire to fall?

S. R. At my own time, in my own place—not in the din of battle, amid the yells of victory.

B. I enjoy the din of battle; and the yells of victory have only to come from pretty lips—!

S. R. Do you mean you actually *like* women?

B. It sounds dreadful, but I should be a brute if I didn't. They've been my consolation.

S. R. They're the luxury of the poor! You can afford natural pleasures. You ought to recognize the fact that your limitations are your liberty.

B. The liberty to love? May I never lose it!

S. R. I shall be glad to assist you to retain it. Remain exactly as you are, and you will.

B. I'm afraid there's very little doubt that I shall remain exactly as I am. I always *have* remained exactly as I am! You make me feel indeed a sort of eternal *tableau vivant*, and inspire me to positively decline to rise. But while I luxuriate in my limitations, as you so happily describe them, what on earth will become of *you?*

S. R. I shall probably succumb to the mockery of my advantages and the ferocity of my pursuers.

B. The real way to escape, my dear man, is to marry.

S. R. (*with a start*). Marry whom?

B. (*diverted, staring*). Anyone you like!

S. R. (*with his hand to his heart*). I thought you meant Miss Jesmond! (*Giving him his hand*) See how my pulse throbs!

B. (*feeling the hand while* S. R. *pants*). You're indeed a wreck!

S. R. (*instinctively, unconsciously wiping his hand with his pocket-handkerchief and going on argumentatively*). You say "anyone I like." But I don't like anyone! I hate them all, and yet they're always *with* me!

B. (*after looking at him an instant with amused compassion*). Let me help you!

S. R. Upon my soul, I think you ought! You've the happy lot—the ideal life: you owe something to others!

B. But what can I do?

S. R. Draw the assailants off—keep them at bay!

B. (*considering, responding, entering into it*). While you gain time—get away? Happy thought! I'll do what I can: I'll cover your retreat.

S. R. I count upon you!

The Album is the only one of these plays in which there is a suggestion of the sort of moral predicament to which James's novels accustom us; the heroine must appear not to love, in order to serve better the man she loves, a motive which is for example of great importance in *The Spoils of Poynton*, written a little later. This play is not the best of the set. *Disengaged*, as a general performance, holds that place; it has the greatest variety of persons, the most skilfully woven plot, and the best final act. Nevertheless *The Album* has the greater interest because it shows James feeling his way towards his own subject. It was written later, and it seems reasonable to assume that having made sufficient progress against his first difficulty, technique, he was experimenting with his second, subject, trying to discover how the situations and characters that really interested him could be worked out in drama. *Guy Domville*, from the sparse accounts available, seems to have been a further step in this direction.

He got no further because of the highly unpleasant circumstances that accompanied the production of this latter work. James was nervous of the event, but failure was not anticipated; prospects and confidences were rather the other way. His first play to be seen, the dramatic version of *The American*, had been produced by Edward Compton at Southport in 1891 and had had a successful run, followed by two months in London. The production of *Guy Domville* in London by George Alexander, with Marion Terry (5 Jan. 1895), was more elaborate. It was on this occasion that hostility was shown; there is even a suspicion that it was organized and malicious. The "incident" is referred to by Shaw.[1] Together with the "ablest" of his colleagues and the "cultivated majority" he applauded the work, and took the "rowdies who brawled" from the gallery to task for their ignorance and bad taste. He sums up: "It will be a deplorable misfortune if *Guy Domville* does not hold the stage long enough to justify Mr. Alexander's enterprise in producing it." James was no lover of a fray, and press pugilism was not his line. "It has been a great relief," he writes, "to feel that one of the most detestable incidents of my life has closed. It has left me with an unutterable horror of the theatre—as well as with a blank uncertainty as to what that horror—bearing on everything that relates to it—will lead me to do in regard to the same—

[1] *Our Theatres in the Nineties*, notice of 12 Jan. 1895. It is described by James himself in a letter of 9 Jan. to William James.

to it, for it, at it, against it!" This affair brought to an abrupt end James's attempts to come to terms with the theatre.[2]

His public behaviour during the scandalous events is said to have been extremely dignified. This is the more to be admired in view of the bitterness of his private remarks. He had thrown himself into the task with such enthusiasm that his disappointment was bound to be great. At the most he felt a certain satisfaction that *Guy Domville* had been appreciated by a few individuals of intelligence and taste. But the "vast English Philistine mob—the regular 'theatrical public' of London," as he describes it, whom he had wooed with a liberality of concession remarkable in so fastidious a person, wouldn't listen to anything worth while. In his half-dozen experiments he had mastered technique only to be thrown out when he used it to good purpose.

The story ends with the Preface to the *Theatricals*. We can scarcely hope to be more luminous about his failure than he is himself, and so we quote a fair passage from it. It is his balance-sheet; a markedly debit statement, presented in a mood of philosophic resignation that turns it into a little masterpiece of fanciful irony:

> The man who pretends to the drama has more to learn, in fine, than any other pretender. . . . The lesson consists for the most part, as the author of these remarks has somewhere else ventured to express the matter, in the periodical throwing overboard of the cargo to save the ship. The ship is always in danger—the most

[2] Some twelve or thirteen years later James again indulged in a short spell of play-writing. Details are given by Percy Lubbock in *Letters of Henry James*. vol. ii. p. 6. The main feature was the production of *The High Bid* at Edinburgh in March 1908 by Forbes-Robertson and his wife. James records in a letter to Henry James, junior (3 April 1908) that "it had a *great* and charming success before a big house at Edinburgh—a real and unmistakable victory." A letter to Mrs. W. K. Clifford (19 July 1909) shows a recrudescence of the old feelings about working for drama and theatre—the sickening process of reducing, compressing, eliminating, but also the fascination that the technical difficulties held for him. In this phase, however, one hears the merest echoes of the earlier agitations and struggles. —It might also be recalled that James dramatized *Daisy Miller* (1882).

successful play has come within an ace of sinking, and the peril recurs every night; so that universal sacrifice is always in the air. The freight, the fittings, the ballast, the passengers, the provisions, the luggage, the crew, the whole thing must inexorably "go," and the vessel is not in proper trim till she is despoiled of everything that might have appeared to make her worth saving; till the last survivor in the last rag of the rigging has been consigned to the fishes, uttering that shriek of despair which lives on in the playwright's ear and becomes eventually the sweetest music he knows. The scientific name of this ferocious salvage is selection—selection made perfect, so that effect, the final residuum, shall become intense—intense with that sole intensity which the theatre can produce and for the sake of which much perhaps will be forgiven it. There is no room in a play for the play itself until everything (including the play, the distracted neophyte pantingly ascertains) has been completely eliminated. Then the fun, as the vulgar phrase is, begins.

Upon this he returns to what he says in one passage is his "legitimate form."

Return to his legitimate form. . . . What then *was* his form? It is strange, it is almost comic, this oscillation between two forms he supposed at different times so positively to be "his," but it gives point to our question, which might at first, in view of the long series of novels from a very copious pen and of the handful of now forgotten dramas, seem to be ridiculous. He was in fact powerfully attracted by drama; but his great embarrassment was the apparatus of the theatre. "Only I feel more and more that I *may* be made for the Drama (God only knows!) but am not made for the theatre!" And again: "The whole odiousness of the thing lies in the connection between the drama and the theatre. The one is admirable in its interest and difficulty, the other loathsome in its conditions. If the drama could only be theoretically or hypothetically acted, the fascination resident in its all but unconquerable (*circumspice!*) form would be unimpaired, and one would be able to have the exquisite exercise without the horrid sacrifice" (to W. James, 29 Dec. 1893). Amidst his greatest enthusiasm for the drama, and his utmost surrender to it, he was never able to forget the advantages of the novel—what the novel could do that drama couldn't, how much more supple an instrument it was for the modern situation, in how many ways, that is to say, it corresponded better to what he in particular was interested in conveying. Distracted by the polar stresses of the two techniques, he ended by combining them, making them more than ever pull in the same direction. From quite early on he had shown a strong tendency to use certain elements of dramatic technique in his novels. After the experiments in play-writing he developed this tendency to its utmost and produced a "drama" freed from the conditions of the stage. With this he really did find the form that was his. He builds a beautiful arch upon the two supports of drama and narrative; and the keystone of the arch is his method of focusing a situation in the mind of one or other of his characters (what is sometimes called, most ambiguously, his "indirect method"). This principle enables him to extend at will an architecture, a "scenic" composition, that he derives essentially from drama; and it gives him the novelist's liberty to elaborate what the playwright can only suggest or refer to. He creates a convention of his own that extends drama and contributes a quite new idea of form to the novel (for this is something different from the early connection of the English novel with the drama). It is all his own creation. Nobody claims him as a dramatist any longer; and the exponents of the novel, Mr. Muir and Mr. Forster for example, qualify their admiration of him as a novelist very severely because they see his technique as a confinement of the novel form. Yet he liberates drama from some of its stricter limitations without losing its power of architecture and of detached statement, and he confines the technique of the novel only to enhance its formal excellence.

There is therefore a closer connection between James's dramatic experiments and the novels that followed than has perhaps been taken notice of. The storm that blew up for him over the theatre is in fact part of a crisis that extends through a decade from about 1889 onwards. It is reflected in most of the works of this period, some of which have apparently nothing to do with his theatre venture. *The Tragic Muse* (1889-90) is plainly relevant, and in two ways. The theatre, the artists who serve it, the public that adores, flatters, reveres, and debases it, belong all on the surface to James's own approaches to it, to all that he found there to attract, tantalize, inspire, and discourage him. But the author has invested his "Tragic Muse" herself, Miriam Rooth, with the character of a representative artist altogether; she embodies the unswerving single-mindedness of the artist, his struggle for expression and technique. She is not only a direct overt tribute to the theatre, but also indirectly a symbol of the artist's struggle James was involved in at this time.

To this period belongs, moreover, the series of ironical stories about the literary life. *The Lesson of the Master*, *The Middle Years*, *The Death of the Lion*, *The Coxon Fund*, *The Next Time*, *The Figure in the Carpet*, were all written contemporaneously with the plays, and it does not seem unreasonable to trace their psychological origin in part at least to the frustrations of the period; to his feeling that his novels were little appreciated, to his unsuccessful efforts at a new kind of writing and at establishing a different relationship as author with a different public. He has referred to these works himself as a kind of "ironic" assertion of the "ideal"; they were assertions imperative to his own faith.

The Other House (1896) belongs to this development, too. Written first as a play, it remains in character and construction very close to a three-act melodrama and contains more plain theatrical violence and excitement, and fewer refinements of perception and treatment, than perhaps any other novel of James.

The two works that bring most clearly the resolution of

James's difficulty are *What Maisie Knew* and *The Spoils of Poynton,* and they appeared in 1896 and 1897, ushering in with a marked assurance the later phase. But his experimenting was not yet concluded. Some three years later appeared *The Awkward Age.* Its chronological position is curious because it does not correspond to the logical line of the experiments. From the latter point of view its position lies between the plays and *The Spoils of Poynton,* for it is his unique attempt at "described drama" on the narrowest terms imaginable. It is a too mechanical transposition of stage scenes. The dialogue is central and it is supported with the minimum description of the persons concerned, a minimum that is very nicely calculated. His idea is to present the picture of the people and their talk; "with no going behind, no *telling about* the figures save by their own appearance and action," as he says in the Preface. The succession of conversations is so spun out, however, and with such a wearisome stuffy confinement to the drawing-room at tea-time, that the work becomes diffuse; and although it has a "pattern," for which James produces wonderfully in the Preface the geometrical equivalent, it ends by losing the intensity and architectonic compactness that was the very thing about dramatic form that was such a bait to James. He limits himself here to the point of extreme rigidity and artificiality without a corresponding gain.

This work brings to a close the decade of James's largest and most crucial experiment in form.

The degree of James's infatuation with the idea of writing plays brings home to one the fact that the dramatic element in his novels is a dominant one. I do not mean only that his *method* is "dramatic," in the subtler senses expounded so interestingly by Percy Lubbock in *The Craft of Fiction.* I mean that his *subjects* are dramatic, and they are more so after *The Tragic Muse* and the experiments in play-writing than they were before. James's love of "predicaments" is common knowledge. A predicament has two aspects, moral and technical. As a moralist James is interested in the problem of behaviour that confronts the fine nature, the resolution that a sensitive virtue will achieve. As an artist the predicament interests him because it is dramatic. In the retrospective glances of the Prefaces, James returns again and again to a favourite prompting of his craftsman's conscience: Dramatize! dramatize! What he came more and more to do was to look for the subject that dramatized itself, the germ that would develop spontaneously according to a dramatic law. Such were his "predicaments"; and the gathering intensity of them—and in consequence the gathering intensity of the technique—can be measured by comparing the dilemma facing Hyacinth Robinson in *The Princess Casamassima* or Nick Dormer in *The Tragic Muse* with that facing Fleda Vetch in *The Spoils of Poynton* or, at the greatest height of all, Maggie Verver in *The Golden Bowl*, and Strether in *The Ambassadors*. And the link between these earlier and later works is to be found in one of the plays, *The Album;* in the predicament of Grace Jesmond, to which we have referred.

Three things tend to obscure the degree of drama present in James's novels: the time element, the subtleties and refinements of the social scene, so opposed to the rapidities and violences of theatre excitement, and finally the psychological detail.

One of his deep-seated objections to stage-drama, amidst all its attractions, was that in the circumstances of the modern world it doesn't give enough time to develop a theme and a situation. An illuminating passage occurs in *The Tragic Muse:*

> He [the dramatist] has to make the basest concessions. One of his principal canons is that he must enable his spectators to catch the suburban trains, which stop at 11.30. What would you think of any other artist—the painter or the novelist—whose governing forces should be the dinner and the suburban trains? The old dramatists didn't defer to them—not so much at least—and that's why they're less and less actable. If they're touched—the large

loose men—it's only to be mutilated and trivialized. Besides, they had a simpler civilization to represent—societies in which the life of man was in action, in passion, in immediate and violent expression. Those things could be put upon the playhouse boards with comparatively little sacrifice of their completeness and their truth. Today we're so infinitely more reflective and complicated and diffuse that it makes all the difference. What can you do with a character, with an idea, with a feeling, between dinner and the suburban trains? You can give a gross, rough sketch of them, but how little you touch them, how bald you leave them! What crudity compared with what the novelist does!

James is here in tune with developments of the age—developments of civilized living, of sensibility, of psychological interest; and not only in tune, but contributing largely to them. It is clear that he is pleading his own case. But it is not only that he thought times and tastes had changed. There is no doubt that James himself, as a person, had a horror of scenes of violence, of the outbreak of passions, of vulgarities in which dignity and manners and civilization, the calm of innocence, the steadfastness of virtue, are sacrificed. But we insist again that he had an acute sense of drama. These elements in his human and artistic nature lead him to a new kind of drama, quite unlike that of the theatre, unsuited to stage conditions, but drama none the less. It is the drama that lurks continually under the surface of civilized manners, without bursting out vehemently. He portrays the subtle pressures, the delicate tensions, the prolonged controlled inner dilemma, the crises that a sense of dignity and propriety prevents from being expressed in crude and devastating forms. His genius more and more makes for the gradual illumination of psychological strains in the relations between a small group of people. And again in doing this, it perfectly suits his book when he takes as his "centres," through whose consciousness he presents the situation, persons of exceptional intelligence or awareness, like Fleda Vetch and Maggie. And if this illumination is gradual, and not precipitate, it none the less refers to an essentially dramatic situation. Quite in the way of drama, it is the imminence of a crisis that starts him off. *The Ambassadors* begins with Strether in Europe investigating a situation that is potentially explosive. *The Golden Bowl* starts with Charlotte, the person from the "past" and the cause of the future crisis, arriving in England on the very eve of Amerigo's marriage to Maggie Verver and coming to see him. There is in these books, particularly after 1895, no chronicling of a life, no "telling the story" of actions, sufferings or love; there is the presentation of a dramatic crisis.

Opening his works with a situation over which the shadow of crisis already hangs, James then elaborates them in such a way as slowly to heighten the tension and maintain it. The maintenance of tension is one of his most distinguishing characteristics, and it appears at its best where the technical alliance between "scenic" composition and the psychological "centre" is closest, as in *The Spoils of Poynton.* Under these conditions he reveals to the full the consciousness and motives of his main characters in all their vital detail and agitation, and develops at its closest and most concentrated the drama of prolonged strains. Under these conditions, too, emerges what is most characteristic and gravely beautiful in James: the fine character, representing, symbolizing, fighting for a *value*—moral or esthetic or both subtly interfused—in opposition to materialism, folly, ugliness and evil.

The technique is seen in its most splendid elaboration and strictness in *The Ambassadors* and *The Golden Bowl.* The latter work, for instance, opens with an "interior monologue" of the Prince followed by four "scenes" of which the Prince is the "centre." He converses with Maggie, there follows a meeting with Fanny Assingham, another with Charlotte Stant, and there is a fourth scene between Fanny and the Colonel her husband; the background to the whole being provided by two events that initiate the crisis: the legal arrangements for the Prince's marriage to Maggie Verver have been completed and he stands on the eve of the wedding; and Charlotte has returned expressly to spend an hour alone with him before his marriage. These scenes form an exposition closely parallel to that of a regular first act; and to re-read them after having read the whole work is to see how they enunciate the principal themes of the book. What follows is an uninterrupted series of modifications, very slight, but very important, of the "dramatic" situation thus expounded. A state of tension is prolonged, and any momentary relaxation only brings a new strain, a redistribution of accent, or a new aspect of the fundamental situation in the reactions of the people concerned. They group and regroup themselves according to a rhythm imposed by a dual force: the initial position, and their characters; and thus they move through a pattern of crisis. Given this new conception of where drama can be found and how presented, and allowing for James's special refinements, he works essentially as a dramatist works, with stress and counter-stress, situation and counter-situation, peripateia, climax and resolution. His fullness is not extended chronicle, teeming incident and pictorial breadth; it is psychological depth. Even incidental aspects derive from a dramatic basis; James's use of the "outsider"—the Maria Gostreys and Fanny Assinghams—is a transformation of the "confidants" of drama, and the Prefaces constantly refer to the use of "ficelles." The great paradox of this extraordinary development is, finally, that as the later works get longer and longer they are more and more dramatic in conception, and more and more concentrated.

James's new creation forces one to reflect again upon the great divisions of literary form, narrative, lyric, and drama. They tend either to be taken for granted, or, nowadays, to be deprecated as irrelevant; though the latter view is more frequently held by the observers rather than the practicians of literary art. Croce, who has done more than anyone else to discredit literary "kinds," is a philosopher. Dilthey, too, the first in Germany to throw the accent on the psychological source of creative work and on "Geistesgeschichte," that is to say, away from the art of the thing, was a philosopher and "Kulturhistoriker."

The remarkable thing about these divisions is in the first place the variety they permit within themselves; and in the second place, perhaps more important still, the extent to which each makes use of the other whilst maintaining its predominant character. They had their origin, as far as the European tradition is concerned, in Greece; and a large emphasis has been placed in recent years on their functional association with the celebrations and ritual of Greek society. But historical and materialist critics have not extended their explanations to the question of the persistence of the forms, in their broad characteristics, under non-Greek conditions. They persist because they have an esthetic origin; it was their *function* that was religious and social. They correspond to predominant ways of experiencing life. They are natural forms, those that life itself suggests, that life itself takes; lyric for states of vision and emotion, narrative for the succession of incident and the pictorial scene, drama for the precipitation of crisis in human relations. They correspond, too, to psychological differences in men.

An important modifying factor in the case of drama has been its association from the beginning with re-enactment. It is the conditions of this that have really determined the *limits* of the form, and indeed its name. It is not merely "action" that is the basis of drama, but a restricted kind of action: action that can be represented by performers in certain conditions of time and place; a severe qualification. Although then, as we have suggested, drama in art corresponds to a recurring phenomenon in life, it is subject to modifying circumstances, and in consequence there remains much in life that is essentially "dramatic" but which is excluded from enactment on a stage. Some aspects of technique present themselves as triumphs wrested from these limitations. The "three unities," as rules of composition, are a willing acceptance of constraint in order to achieve more brilliant feats of *art*. They involve the utmost concentration on the crisis, at the price of a certain artificiality and with the sacrifice of subjects that do not admit of compression. Elizabethan dramatists were freer in handling time and place. But even so their freedom is only relative, there is a point beyond which it is impossible to go; there remain subjects that cannot be made to conform to stage conditions.

Life is infinite and art by comparison confined. But a principal feature of its evolution is the gradual extension of its capacity to meet this infinite variety of life; to modify existing forms, or—much more rarely—create new ones that give it the mastery of further territories of life so far withheld from it. This general law holds good for the relations between crisis in life and crisis in dramatic art. There is a limitless range of the former, and many aspects of it have not been brought within the capacity of traditional stage-drama. Henry James has exploited in a form that is subtly compounded of two techniques one of the varieties of drama that life holds, and the stage cannot.

This solution of James's is a feat of genius because it saves so large a part of his outfit as a writer; it restores to him, in however disguised a form, the novelist's liberty of comment and description. It is tempting sometimes to regret his departure from the theatre, to look upon him as an early victim of the struggle to reconcile the theatre again with poetry and style. We recall Shaw's tribute to James on the score of *Guy Domville* (coming from an aggressive personality of such opposed tastes, one of the most touching things in criticism). We recall his repeated chivalrous mention of James as one of those whom drama needed for its art but whom the public wouldn't have. And we might find ourselves deploring conditions that admitted no poetry, no refinement, no intelligence, no style, no James; accusing an audience that had so little care for standards. To do so, however, would be to suppose that his failure in the theatre was alone responsible for his leaving it, and that his new form was something undertaken as a compensating substitute. Nothing could be more absurd in face of works in which the form matches so perfectly the subject. It is impossible to imagine a form of stage-drama in which James could have expressed adequately all he had to say. Many of his qualities of mind and sensibility could obviously not have been expressed in the dialogue of plays. The simple proof is to be found in that of his novels. Lively, supple, terse, graceful, refined, intelligent–it is remarkable; yet it is only half of what James has to give. The other half contains his descriptive excellences; often spare and economical but always vivid; unobtrusive, but always there, woven in. It contains his abundant comment; the wealth of detailed observation–of thoughts, reflexions, reactions, motives, feelings, judgements, visual and aural impressions–gathered into sentences that are flexible and fluid, responding easily to the continual flow of impression and idea, but never collapsing into disorder. No convention of drama at that time could have given James scope for all the rays of light he was to project on life, society, and behaviour, as he allowed his observation and judgement to play upon them. Dialogue in a prose play could not contain the imagery that becomes more and more of the very essence of the later works, an imagery that is no catching at the "poetic" but always a spontaneous clarification of his idea. The few attempts he makes at working out a metaphor in dialogue (there is one in the passage quoted above from *The Album*) are too forced for the effect to be faultless.

If James's excursion into stage-drama was an aberration, it bore the finest fruits. It was for James, as part of an experiment, the failure that cleared the way for success. For art it found a form of drama inaccessible to the theatre and capable of a more satisfactory alliance with psychology, one of the profoundest new influences of the time, than contemporary prose realist drama. The three forces of his inspiration—the sense of moral crisis, the architecture and direct presentation of drama, the analysis of behaviour and manners—found in his unique final form their balanced and adequate expression. This combination, so remarkable in James, was the fruit of his struggle with the temptation of the theatre, of his own predicament as an artist. And when he brings to an end the Preface to *The Ambassadors* with the conviction "that the Novel remains still, under the right persuasion, the most independent, most elastic, most prodigious of literary forms," his thought proceeds from his deepest intuitions. For he means that it is elastic enough to be used for presenting a dramatic subject independently of the conditions of re-enactment, a drama, in short, that won't go on a stage. And what could be more "prodigious" than that?

GRILLPARZER

GRILLPARZER belongs to a development of drama that started with Lessing about the middle of the eighteenth century and ended with Hebbel a little more than a hundred years later. It is a remarkable phase of the art. In the first place, half a dozen writers of importance contributed to it—Lessing, Schiller, Goethe, Grillparzer, Büchner, and Hebbel. In the second place, they wrote for the most part in verse, revitalizing the great European tradition of dramatic poetry that was at its best in the sixteenth and seventeenth centuries and of which Voltaire and Marivaux were the decadent representatives in the eighteenth. And they continued this tradition in Germany during a period when it was extinct in the rest of Europe. Their work owes its existence in a general way to the most astonishing literary phenomenon of the eighteenth century: the rapid development of German literature from a state of imitation and crudity to one of maturity, variety, and splendour, unrivalled in Europe at the end of the century. Romanticism here coincided with a late Renaissance and a classical humanism. The consequence was that poetry and writing generally had the greatest range and diversity of character. The poetic inspiration of the pre-eminent writers had too large a compass to be contained in lyric alone. They were profoundly acquainted, it is true, with the realm of feeling, they knew as well as anybody, and even better, exaltations and aspiration. But they were absorbed, too, like the dramatic poets of the sixteenth and seventeenth centuries, by the analysis of passion and character, by the vision of men in action; and they sought deliberately to understand the universal aspects of human behaviour. Such interests took Goethe and Schiller to the dramatic form. We shall refer later to certain limitations of German drama which they share; but their powerful genius and a spontaneous enthusiasm for the theatre enabled them to produce a series of great plays. Shakespeare was an important early influence; later they studied Greek and French models, and something of each passed into their writing. But more important perhaps than precise traceable influences of this kind was a consciousness that verse-drama was the ideal form of literary expression. Lessing no doubt contributed to this conception, for he held that human actions were the worthiest subject of poetry, and verse-drama was a purer and intenser form than narrative. It may be a symptom of the very late poetic maturity of Germany that a form should be so singled out as pre-eminent, that it should be lighted upon not merely by a spontaneous creative gift but also by a scholarly judgement weighing one form against another in the achievements of the past. It may be that something of this sort must happen when a form has decayed. Goethe and Schiller both wrote their first plays in prose and then adopted verse to suit a more elevated conception. In doing so they are only the first modern example of poets deliberately re-creating verse-drama as an act of literary judgement and imposing it in opposition to current theatre entertainment.

This in itself might be sufficient to give German drama the literary flavour that distinguishes it, for example, from the Elizabethan. Other factors contributed. Goethe had indisputably the power to create living characters, but he rarely confined himself to a pure dramatic aim, and it puts a gulf between him and writers like Shakespeare and Racine. His *Iphigenie auf Tauris* uses a dramatic action to give an image of nobility. *Torquato Tasso* is a piece of self-analysis. *Faust* elaborates a philosophical idea. Schiller, on his side, was always as much a preacher as a dramatist. He was a passionate idealist, a reformer by temperament, and the note that strikes one in all his writings—poems, dramas, or essays—as characteristic is that of the orator. But his gifts were mixed and amongst them were an acute sense of the theatre and a rapidly developed mastery of dramatic technique ("ein Meister der Spannung und des bewegten Spiels," Gundolf calls him). These gifts he used largely to illuminate ideas and propagate his ideals. As a dramatist he is therefore a most tantalizing figure. How great his creative powers were can be seen from *Wallenstein,* in which, under the influence of Goethe and the Greeks, a maximum of presentation and a minimum of oratory is achieved. As a piece of dramatic art, it is his finest; but it is less characteristic of his mind, and perhaps less powerful, than *Don Carlos* or *Wilhelm Tell,* because in these he is more consistent with himself. His own particular greatness, which lay in his moral nature, finds here more adequate expression.

The drama created by Goethe and Schiller has thus certain features which distinguish it sharply from previous work by authors of comparable powers. Schiller was, moreover, quite frank in his didactic approach to the theatre; he saw what it might, as an institution, do towards the moral education of the wider public, and he pressed it with unashamed enthusiasm into that service. These things left their mark on the whole tradition.

We might cavil at this didacticism. With the Elizabethans and the Spaniards and the French clsasical writers in our memory, we feel that drama suffered when ideas became more important than presentation. It is, however, only fair to add that the most distinguished dramatists in Europe in the nineteenth century, with one or two exceptions, did the same, and did it less well.

✦

Grillparzer was one of these exceptions. Born in Vienna in 1791, he grew up in a literary atmosphere dominated by Goethe, Schiller and the romantic school. Shakespeare and the Spanish dramatists were translated, and Schlegel's lectures on the drama, covering all the great periods, were given in Vienna in 1808. In 1814, moreover, Joseph Schreyvogel became playwright and secretary to the famous Burgtheater and made history with his productions of Shakespeare and the Spanish dramatists.

It was Grillparzer's good fortune that dramatic poetry had established itself; the verse convention was in existence, it had a prestige, it could be developed. It is his particular distinctinction that amongst the writers, from Lessing to Hebbel, who used this form, he is the one who uses it in the purest artistic spirit, with the least admixture of ideas. It would be wrong to say that he was entirely without a didactic strain. But it only appears later in his life, and principally in plays that were written in retirement from active connections with the theatre. The morals and politics of *Libussa* and *Ein Bruderzwist in Habsburg* are a bequeathal of the ageing poet's wisdom to his fellow-countrymen. In the plays that are characteristic of his genius at its best the dominating feature is poetic singlemindedness, an insistent devotion to the purest and most intense dramatic statement. His Austrian temperament and the atmosphere of Vienna may have had a large influence on his artistic aims. The place had a metropolitan character that no city in Germany could claim to equal. There was sociability and the desire for entertainment. There was an aristocratic society, proverbially gay, taking its pleasures lightly, and more disposed to sensuous enjoyments than the brooding pedantic people of the north. It is a city of baroque art; there is little Gothic. In such an atmosphere the theatre was popular. Drawing its support from all sections of the population, it secured an audience that took a spontaneous delight in the imagination without needing austere precepts to justify its pleasures. Writers like Raimund and Nestroy testify to the strength of a native tradition, to the give-and-take that existed between dramatist and audience. Grillparzer was later to have tiffs with this audience; but he springs from it. It appears quite natural, too, that a native of the city of German-speaking lands that owes most to the Mediterranean tradition should find himself at home above all with the Spaniards Calderon and particularly Lope de Vega; more than with Shakespeare, especially the Shakespeare transmitted by *Sturm und Drang* and romanticism. For though these two parties saw Shakespeare in somewhat different ways, they were yet at one in admiring above all a poet who in their view quite transcended the form he worked in; they were most enthusiastic where he most transcended. Grillparzer, in quite a different spirit, admired Shakespeare and the Spaniards because of their superlative qualities as dramatists.

The first play of his to be produced, *Die Ahnfrau* (1817), has its roots far more clearly in theatrical art than the first attempt of either Schiller or Goethe. *Die Räuber* and *Götz von Berlichingen* have great dramatic merits, and they are both more important literary works than *Die Ahnfrau;* but the power of the first lies in its revolutionary spirit, and the principal merit of the second is its vividness as a historical tableau. Neither of these characteristics is specifically of drama alone. *Die Ahnfrau* is fantastic, but its effects are essentially and in the best sense theatrical. It is melodramatic, but that is a failure in quality not in kind. Its tragic plot is far-fetched and mechanical, like the "fatalistic horror-dramas" of the time; but its poetic promise is quite brilliant and evokes something like genuine tragic feeling in spite of extravagances, and does so with the intensity that is achieved in the theatre alone.

Hostile critics excited Grillparzer's peevishness by ignoring the poetic merits of his piece and ascribing its success solely to its more lurid effects. The sting to his artistic vanity produced one of the motives for his next work: he records that he wanted to show himself capable of treating a quite simple subject and developing all his dramatic effects from character and emotional conflict. The *Sappho* material, suggested by a friend who wanted him to write an opera text, gave him the subject he was looking for. The tragedy was written down in four weeks. It is so fine and characteristic, that the vindication is complete; the qualities that he was accused of lacking turn out to be the ones that make him remarkable.

Sappho, feeling amidst her triumphs as a poet her isolation as a woman and an ordinary mortal, longs for a simple human love and domestic happiness. She chooses Phaon to be her husband, only to find that his feeling for her is admiration and reverence for the poet in her; the love she craves for he gives to her slave Melitta. Grillparzer shows admirably how the situation forces her into all the indignities that a jealous woman suffers and commits, whilst Phaon, seeing more and more clearly the gulf set between them, drives her back into the elevated sphere that is hers alone, that of poetic inspiration. The man from whom she wanted life gives her back to poetry. The appeals to her humanity, her dignity, her nobility, force her to accept the union of Phaon and Melitta; but she commits suicide. This action is of the simplest and devoid of purely theatrical sensations. It consists of a single mental conflict developed to its tragic conclusion, and in fact there is such a concentration on a quite simple relationship between only three persons, and such a relatively small amount of stage business, that it is easy to underestimate the degree of action the play contains and overlook the dramatic quality of many passages that to a superficial view might seem merely meditative or lyrical.

The insistence, in this play, on the opposition between art and life is a product of romanticism. To the legendary picture of Sappho as a type of the subjective lyric rhapsodist

Grillparzer has added traits from the ideas of the German romantics on poets and poetry; the poet as a depersonalized medium of the ranging Spirit, his utterance the response of an aeolian harp to the breath of divinities. As a man of flesh and blood, a social being, a son, husband, father, a wage-earner, he had no importance for this view, existing only as the theatre of action for the autonomous and liberated fancy. From this derives an air of idealism and romanticism that is undoubtedly one of the charms of the piece; and it might be easy to fall into the error of supposing that Grillparzer aims chiefly at glorifying the romantic conception of the poet as a being elevated above ordinary mortal life, using the tragic situation to intensify a glory of martyrdom. His handling of the subject shows, however, that his interest does not lie in such an idealization, but rather in the human drama; and the implications of the treatment make it clear that he is critical of the romantic attitude.

For the foundation of the play is the longing of Sappho to be linked with life; and the dramatic treatment is dominated by the motive of jealousy. It is the most pregnant motive he could have used to show his heroine in conflict with life; and he uses it largely and powerfully so that the jealousy action is the very substance of what is put before the spectator. That is to say his dramatic interest in her is the human, not the ideal one. Sappho is a poet, and that is very wonderful and dignified; but she is tragic because she is a woman as well as a poet. This gives the play a human poignancy that it could never have had as a mere play about a poetess, as homage to a poetic ideal.

The starting-point for the author is, then, a poet isolated by her vocation from ordinary life and wishing to overcome the barrier; but the drama is a portrayal of passion. Taking a poetess as his heroine, Grillparzer develops the woman in her for the action of his play. Starting off with something that might easily have remained a lyrical tribute to an idea, he puts in the foreground the human passion and becomes a dramatist. Beginning with an atmosphere of romantic poetry and idealism, he treats the subject with a psychological realism that amongst his contemporaries he alone possessed.

This gives the play a particular significance in the history of the relations between poetry and drama. For what makes Grillparzer a dramatist makes him a critic of the romantic conception of the poet, that is, of the contemporary ideal. If he had accepted this latter he could not have created the character of Sappho, who wants *life*, and freedom from poetic-sacerdotal office; and if he had been a romantic himself of the same type he would not have commanded the knowledge of life, passion, motive, good and evil that makes the dramatist. *Sappho* is the first objective analysis of the position of the romantic poet divorced from life, the first critical diagnosis—always in the form of dramatic statement—of a pathological condition of poets and poetry arising from romanticism.

The following play, *Das Goldene Vlies* (a trilogy), establishes completely the artistic identity of Grillparzer that we see emerging in *Sappho* from influences foreign to it. Its substance is psychological analysis of Medea's relations with Jason, with an implicit criticism of another aspect of romanticism, the romantic "hero."

We see in this and the later plays Grillparzer's determined effort at "Gestalt"; his elimination of all ideas except the poetic one. Here are the fruits of a deliberate struggle waged against the confusion of philosophy with poetry in much of the writing of his time and in much German writing altogether; and how consciously he pursued his aim can be seen in his notes on criticism and esthetics. No German writer has such incisive things to say about the poetic malpractices of his countrymen. To say about a Latin writer that he aimed at "form" would be on the whole a superfluous statement; to say it about the German Grillparzer is a necessary critical compliment. He is unique for his devotion to the value of dramatic statement as a sufficient one in itself, without subservience to a philosophical idea. Of all German dramatists, Grillparzer is the one who was least obsessed with Shakespeare; but he is the nearest to him in artistic temper.

There is, however, a further reason why we can properly insist on his sensitiveness as an artist. It is because his ideal of dramatic poetry was about to be submerged in Europe generally for almost a century. Hebbel, Dumas fils, and Ibsen were very shortly afterwards, under the compulsion of a new intellectual climate, to buy vitality for drama at the cost of its esthetic integrity. Grillparzer was the last dramatist to work in the high Renaissance tradition, the last for a very long time to produce a creation that has formal purity.

Given this artistic single-mindedness, the originality of Grillparzer lies in a particular psychological illumination of his subject, and the devising of a technique to this end. There is of course in every play a psychological groundwork. But the novelty in Grillparzer is that it is more than a matter of groundwork. Psychology becomes an aim in itself, our attention is directed explicitly to it as a new interest. In some editions of *Das Goldene Vlies* the following motto appears at the head of the play:

> L'on a remarqué que la plupart des hommes sont, dans le cours de leur vie, souvent dissemblables à euxmêmes, et semblent se transformer en des hommes tout différents. (Rousseau, *Confessions*, IX.)

I do not know whether this is Grillparzer's own quotation or that of an editor; but it is certainly apt. The result in this work is a new interpretation of the Medea subject. The central character loses the heroic simplicity of the figure of the myth, and becomes a complex person, presented in a much more human and intimate light. She is shown as the victim of a Jason who changes. He woos her as the brilliant leader of the Argonaut heroes, self-assertive and exuberant; but at home in Greece, the days of adventure over, he despises the woman from Colchis. The tragedy of inconstancy is supported by the psychological study of a barbarian woman who, in spite of efforts to adapt herself, remains a stranger in Greece. Grillparzer achieves his new interpretation through a remarkable invention of situation and incident. Any elaboration of psychology demands a great deal of self-revelation in speeches both in monologue and dialogue, and Grillparzer's verse makes the most of the drama of speech, though his use of monologue in this and succeeding works is very sparing. But his peculiar technical power and originality lies in a wealth of revealing incident. His invention never fails him, and he manages, too, with a very moderate use of scene-change. One could give many examples, because it is the author's essential method; but one of the best is in the third act of *Die Argonauten*, the second play of the trilogy. The whole act, which is the pivot of the work, is a portrayal of Medea's mental conflict. It is not sufficient to say that every external incident is used for a particular purpose; the corollary must also be stated, that the phases of the mental conflict in its continuous and subtle modification are illustrated by an adequate number of external incidents. Medea's resistance to Jason to the point of fighting him; her weakness when he disarms himself and challenges her to kill him; her silence when she has surrendered; her sudden revolt; her emotion when her father comes; and then her cry when Jason makes as if to leave her for ever—these are all incidents, presented continuously and naturally, which reflect turns and convulsions of feeling in Medea. Caught between the parties to the conflict, her love has to struggle with her piety and with her overwhelming fear that the crime previously committed by her father against the Greeks is already close to being avenged. A climax of intense irony is reached when, Medea having given herself over to

Jason and incurred her father's curse, Jason's first act is to demand the way to recover the fleece—the symbol of wrong-doing—from her father. It is a state of mind that is depicted, and Grillparzer finds at every point the external incident that reveals it. His plays are thus remarkable for the way in which they achieve continuous psychological illumination with a variety of outward incident.

Grillparzer's new kind of interest in psychology enables him to develop in a new way the tradition of Goethe and Schiller that he takes up. The assumptions of their work remain to a large extent those of his own: the subject from legend, myth and history; the verse-form of drama; the effort towards universality. But he would not be so interesting if he had not shown that the instrument created by them was capable of further use, even in a period dominated almost completely by lyric and not dramatic inspiration. He was himself not strong enough as a poet to make significant innovations of language or verse-form, and his facility in writing led often to slovenly workmanship in the detail of versification. The one verse-form that he alone uses is the trochaic line of four accents that he found in Spanish dramatists, but he uses it in his two weakest productions (*Die Ahnfrau* and *Der Traum ein Leben*), whilst in all his major works he adheres to blank verse. But there was no special need for him to devise new verse-forms. His powers were sufficient to enable him to use well a form that was to hand, and to maintain its vitality by adding a new interest.

From the European point of view Grillparzer is one of the first authors for whom a picture of the mental process determines composition; for whom psychology does not primarily support the picture of the actions of a particular character, as in Shakespeare, but becomes in increasing degree itself the object of portrayal. His originality in this respect has not, I think, been sufficiently recognized. He was writing his plays a little earlier than Stendhal was writing *Le Rouge et le Noir* and *La Chartreuse de Parme*. To Stendhal falls the credit of having initiated the "psychological novel," anticipating by fifty years a characteristic interest of the modern era. That interest was in fact to find more adequate expression in the novel; indeed, the development of the psychological theme goes hand in hand with a greater refinement of the novel-form, a point we discuss in connection with T. S. Eliot and Henry James. Grillparzer owes much of his success to his historical position. He is early enough to benefit by the poetry of Goethe and Schiller, to assume naturally their conventions and take from them the elevated outlook and poetic conception. And he is late enough to sense the beginnings of a new way of looking at human beings, a closer and subtler investigation of emotions and passions in their origin and expression; something that is no longer eighteenth century, or romantic, but essentially of the spirit of the middle and the later nineteenth century.

Das Goldene Vlies shows Grillparzer's technique applied to a long history and a complex material. *Des Meeres und der Liebe Wellen* shows it used in support of a subject of extreme simplicity. There is no drama in German literature that is so exclusively a poetic handling of the theme of tragic love, so purely directed to the portrayal of emotion; no work in which love in its simplest aspect as human passion is the theme and content, and not merely an erotic interest incidental to some other theme, as in Schiller's *Don Carlos*, or Goethe's *Torquato Tasso*, or *Faust*.

It is the play of Grillparzer which has the least external action and the fewest agents of tension. But it maintains the interest without a break by the delicacy with which the growth of Hero's love is presented. Already in love, she remains still the chaste priestess; still the priestess, she has already laid off the sacred office and assumed the rights of a mortal in love. The atmosphere is heavy with the sweetness of a desire that has not yet reached the acts of passion; it is forbidden, but still innocent. Hero's love, initiated at the moment she takes her vows, is doomed to a tragic end, but the inevitable catastrophe is suspended for a short space of time during which we are spectators of the most exquisite phase of love, its awakening. This suggestion of the idyllic within tragic circumstances gives the work its unique beauty.

Common to these plays is an implicit criticism of romantic illusion. Grillparzer's psychological realism, the foundation of his power as a dramatist, is a faculty that prevents him from being, like his contemporaries, simply a romantic. To expose the illusion, however, he has to portray it: Sappho the romantic poet, Jason the romantic hero, Medea exotically alluring, the perfect romantic love of Hero and Leander. The essence of these tragedies is the tension between romantic dream and the real restraints of living; the dream is subjected to a realist analysis, but all the music and poetry of romanticism is woven in. In a later play, *Der Traum ein Leben*, half fairy-tale, half morality, Grillparzer openly preaches against vain dreams of heroic adventure, of wealth and power and fame, and recommends the contentment of the common round and the domestic task for true happiness. But he loses his power when he turns didactic. His message, directly stated, sounds insipid and somewhat morosely disillusioned. His poetic powers were greatest where he was the pure dramatic artist.

Grillparzer's dramas on historical subjects illustrate the range of his observation and technical powers. They fall into two classes: those which are historical in a real sense, and those in which the historical subject is merely conventional. The latter do not differ essentially from other plays such as those we have considered. In *Ein Treuer Diener seines Herrn*, for example, and *Die Jüdin von Toledo*, the characters are royal and noble persons, the scene palaces and state chambers;

but the theme is character, the conflict personal, almost domestic. The former is a tragedy of loyalty in a king's servant, love, jealousy, and intrigue its propulsive force. The latter is a study of moral laxity breaking out suddenly in a king whose early manhood was spent under exceptional discipline in service to the state. The interest lies always in the interplay more of private character and situation than of public personality and historical event.

König Ottokars Glück und Ende is rather different. Its subject is the defeat of Ottokar, king of Bohemia, at the hands of Rudolf, the founder of the Habsburg line, and it has in it more of the movement of history proper than any other work of the same author; the only comparable one might be the very late *Ein Bruderzwist in Habsburg*, which, however, is much inferior. The sense of state affairs and political action that we find in Shakespeare and Schiller is to be found here. Grillparzer has himself recorded that the complex material gave him trouble. He surmounted the difficulties, however, with the greatest skill, showing himself almost the equal of Schiller in his technical mastery of a mass of historical character and events. Yet the play, in spite of its power and breadth and fine detail, is not satisfactory in its total effect, and a reason might be found in the dual source of its inspiration. It is sentimental history mixed up with Grillparzer's main interest, psychology; patriotic glorification of the Habsburg monarchy mingling with the study of a "great man" at the height of his power and in his decline. However much he disliked some of the ways of government under the Metternich system, Grillparzer's loyalty to the Habsburgs and their imperial rule was unquestioned and sincere, and so his piece is genuine and not a mere act of flattery. One notices, too, that his portrait of Rudolf, the founder of the dynasty, is to such an extent a picture of wise and just rulership that his play embodies precepts for an imperial house as well as homage to one. But this kind of history was not as original as some other things Grillparzer could do; it was an overflow from romanticism, and in Grillparzer it is interesting chiefly as an application to *Austrian* history of a particular aspect of romantic feeling. The history, however, spoils the tragedy. The right and wrong that generate the conflicts of a tragic character are here distributed over two persons: Ottokar and Rudolf. Rudolf is right; Ottokar is wrong. The latter forfeits our sympathy, and Grillparzer's grandiose conception of a tragic hero on the Napoleonic scale breaks down over the tribute to the Habsburg. Grillparzer's homage was ill-timed. The Habsburg reigning at that moment being anxious not to offend his Czech subjects, the reward the piece got for its patriotism was to be held back for two years by the censorship.

For Austrian national sentiment the expression of Grillparzer's predilections in history and politics is a merit in *König Ottokars Glück und Ende*. Other readers may feel it to be rather an obtrusion, though it is evidence of the poet's breadth.

Grillparzer's Austrian nationality is, however, interesting to the European reader from a quite different and less obvious point of view. The nations of Europe who in the past achieved imperial or continental domination, that is those who have shown great political capacity, England and France, and we might add Spain, all produced a drama that is a vivid picture of men, of human character and passions; a drama of great penetration in its accurate and dispassionate analysis of life, its power of statement, its vision of impersonal reality. Germany has never developed the qualities necessary for political rulership; material force is relied upon to replace the art of governing men through knowledge of man. And Germany has no drama comparable in impersonal statement to that of England, France or Spain. Its literature has not been fed to the same extent from the world of action and will, its drama and novel have not emerged from the observation of society and the political arena, but in spite of them. The characteristic creation of Germany in the field of the novel, for instance, is the *Bildungsroman*, the *Wilhelm Meister* type of work that records intellectual development in an individual. The springs of the best German poetry are in dreams, speculations, and the personal search for metaphysical experiences. In poetry they are greatest in romantic lyric; their golden age of literature is the romantic period of Europe. They excel in music, the most abstract art. Lacking a fine touch for reality, they expand the inner life, detached from the outer. Impatient of learning the art of social living, they substitute a mental fiction for the real world and find in it what they call transcendent truth and true freedom. To say this is not to detract from their achievement; where their inspiration is sincere and deep, its products are great and they express one phase of our existence. But there is a restriction and a gap. These considerations seem to find an illustration in Grillparzer. In poetic power, in the creative use of language, he is inferior to the lyric poets of the great periods–Novalis, Hölderlin, George, Rilke; inferior even to a prose rhapsodist like Herder. But in his sense of reality he is unique, if we except the rather special case of Goethe. It may be that his Austrian nationality has something to do with it; for Austria, as the centre of power of the Holy Roman Empire and later the Austro-Hungarian, came nearer to political success than the modern German Reich has ever done.

Grillparzer is, then, an extremely important link in the development of drama in Germany and Europe. From a purely German point of view he is distinguished by his freedom from the obtrusiveness of ideas that so often spoils the form of German dramatic writing, by the way he devotes himself to the poet's task of presentation. His work has also the distinction of a closer organic link with the theatre, of being more in and of it, than is the case with most of his northern compatriots. There can be no doubt that Goethe and Schiller simply imposed their mature work on the theatre and its public. They dictated ideals and standards. Schiller maintained a contact with the crowd, perhaps, because of his powerful sense of the theatrical, his ideal flights being acceptable when undertaken on the wings of melodrama. But plays like *Iphigenie auf Tauris* and *Torquato Tasso*, wonderful poems that they are, are royal dispensations to the theatre; they are scarcely its own fruits. Grillparzer was a lesser intellect and a lesser poet than either of these two. But he had a combination of gifts which in their balance made him a more satisfying poet of the theatre. It is also worth recalling that he made one of the very few contributions to high comedy in the whole of German literature.

From the European point of view, Grillparzer's work is notable for two principal reasons. He continues with a great measure of success the creation of dramatic poetry begun by his eminent predecessors, making a large contribution to what is, in spite of our reservations, a significant achievement of German literature: to have revitalized the drama–drawing on all the great lessons of the past to do so, the Greeks, Shakespeare, the French, the Spaniards–during a period that was barren in the rest of Europe. And secondly he is important historically, because in the realist spirit of his psychological analysis we observe a consciousness that is new in nineteenth-century literature.

HEBBEL

HEBBEL is a lesser artist than Grillparzer; but such is the magnetic hold of abstract ideas over the German mind that his countrymen have always accounted him the more important poet. Those who accuse Grillparzer of shallowness because they cannot find in his art a religion or a "Weltanschauung" turn with relief to Hebbel's profundities; and the name of "Grübler"—the man who broods and broods—that Hebbel earned for himself loses on their lips any critical reservation it might imply and becomes simple homage. Perhaps it is the rank given him by his countrymen that explains why he has been translated into English and assigned his niche in the Everyman Library, whilst Grillparzer remains comparatively unknown.

It can of course be said that if Hebbel brooded, and so weakened his art, he yet brooded greatly. Apologists will always be needed, but they will always be able to make out a strong case for him. His dramatic project may offend a pure canon; but it is ambitious enough to be interesting. Some of his problems are morbid, but others are of general value. The powerful technique which he uses to exemplify them is, moreover, another reason why he can often rally an attention that becomes unwilling and refractory.

Hebbel started his play-writing career amidst the events of the thirties and forties of last century; he was born in 1813, and his first play, *Judith*, appeared in 1841. It was a political age, and the energies of literature were in great part directed towards the general ferment. All was preparation for revolution, and liberal hopes ran high. Hebbel was immensely influenced by this age; not, however, so much by its detailed policies, one way or the other, as by its character. The dominant striking feature was the fact of conflict, the immediacy of change, the reality of transition. Drawing back, the better to contemplate, Hebbel saw all the appearances of men seeking a different foundation for their individual and social life, either through new institutions or through revitalizing existing ones. He links his speculative awareness of the character of the age with his own creative impulses, which were towards drama. He sees a time of crisis as the condition of drama, an epoch of change providing the dialectic (his own word) on which drama depends. He pictures the dramatist as the analyst of his age, tracing the causes of conflict, clarifying the moral conceptions that are changing, discovering the essential structure, the essential drama, of the time and representing it in "powerful images" (gewaltige Bilder).

These ideas were put forward by Hebbel in the Preface he wrote in 1844 for the tragedy *Maria Magdalena*, and the work is a straightforward illustration of them. The moral atmosphere is that of the most fanatic and narrow bourgeois code of respectability and virtue, of which Meister Anton is the incarnation, and which is characteristic of the mid-nineteenth century. When his daughter Klara is forsaken by her lover, fear of her father's rigid puritanism drives her to commit suicide rather than face the shame of bearing her child. The challenge of the piece, made explicit at the close, is to a larger charity and liberality of moral outlook. The suggestion is that such a change of outlook will come, and Klara therefore appears as a tragic victim of a moral code that is absolute for her father, but relative for Hebbel; she is as much the victim of time as of her father.

The contemporary directness of the theme of *Maria Magdalena* makes it clear that Hebbel is treading a path parallel to that Dumas fils entered upon a little later, and to the still broader way opened by Ibsen a few years after Hebbel's death. Both the play and its preface are from this point of view prophetic. The succeeding decades confirmed Hebbel's interpretation. They brought the theory of evolution, the expansion of historical knowledge and scientific research, the disintegration of religious belief, the beginnings of "socialist" thought. These developments showed a major change in the values of European society, and they were followed closely by an outburst of drama that stood in the strictest relationship to them. Hebbel's play is not what afterwards came to be known as "social problem drama"; but it is a precursor of that movement because of its criticism of the moral outlook of the bourgeoisie.

But after *Maria Magdalena* Hebbel avoids contemporary subject-matter and turns to history and legend. In doing so his motive seems to have been the keenest desire to avoid the ephemeral and keep himself detached from mere polemics of the moment. His theme, however, remains the same: historical moments in which moralities clash. In a succession of plays—*Herodes und Mariamne*, *Gyges und sein Ring*, *Agnes Bernauer*—he produces a grandiose generalization of his idea. The particular criticism of a contemporary belief is relinquished for dramatic symbols that refer indirectly to his analysis of his own age. Each of these works portrays a conflict of moral outlook; they are examples from history akin to the contemporary example of *Maria Magdalena*. And the conflict is always treated so as to suggest a large historical background, the emergence of a new idea that will transform society.

In choosing this method Hebbel is aiming—somewhat too consciously—at the utmost universality of statement. Ibsen, for instance, treated different aspects of the contemporary conflict, adding particular to particular and point to point in his broad attack on bourgeois morals; and each time he is absorbed by the particular problem. Proceeding realistically, he has different plays for different ideas. Hebbel, proceeding by symbolical reference, gives different illustrations of *one* idea: the emergence of a new outlook, the historical dialectic that it involves. He represents a conflict that varies in particulars but is essentially the same. It is, stated in broad terms, the struggle between a view that is advanced, progressive, more liberal and human, and one that is conservative, retrogressive, confined and barbarous. It is the drama of progress towards civilization. Mariamne asserts her conception of personal dignity against the tyranny of Herod which has no respect for human persons. Kandaules, with a vision of men liberated from superstitions, offends the moral prejudices of his wife Rhodope. Agnes Bernauer and Albrecht fight for their love against the inhumanity of class distinctions. Mariamne dies; Kandaules dies; Agnes dies; all sacrificed to the more primitive outlook. These works are imbued with the sense of moral evolution. They are a dramatization of that process, both separately and in their cumulative effect.

On the face of it so bold a conception is highly original and compels admiration; Hebbel's dispositions are magnificent. The actual performance raises some critical doubts. For the method involved him in a serious difficulty that he was not able to surmount, hard as he tried. In presenting a particular clash of belief in a remote age and place, as, for instance, in *Gyges und sein Ring*, the material itself forced upon him a certain degree of historical verisimilitude; the quarrel between Kandaules and Rhodope is one that concerns customs of their time and locality. But it is impossible to maintain interest in a clash of opinions which on both sides belong to past history; and our reaction to the play certainly suffers from this fact. The larger implication, the reference to his own time, is bought too dearly at the cost of tedious detail. On the other hand, when he makes the clash of opinions as general as possible in order to maintain the liveliest contemporary implications, Hebbel falls into the opposite defect of abstraction. He is always in one or the other of these two false positions; indeed he is generally in both at once. Either he has particulars which leave us unmoved, or he makes his general idea apparent at the expense of poetic vividness. The fault lies in the preponderance of an abstract idea. His plays, in the last resort, are not visions or statements of life, but illustrations, selected and adjusted, of an intellectual analysis.

Hebbel was in fact caught in a sharp dilemma. His interest in history shows him in tune with a marked feature of his time. Hegel was the commanding philosopher; and historians of every branch of human activity were beginning to multiply. But the increasing historical knowledge of the nineteenth century, the motive of which was scientific accuracy, made the historical drama impossible. Schiller was still able to write "historical" dramas on seventeenth and eighteenth century assumptions; that is to say, using historical events and persons for a drama that was valid by its humanity, as with Shakespeare and Racine. Grillparzer, too, clings in the main to the same foundation, though something new, the colouring of romantic patriotism, is creeping in. Hebbel is beyond the reach of both attitudes. History is no longer humanity, no longer an object of romantic feeling; it is itself. Hebbel's peculiar position is that he wants to use drama to convey a view of history at the very moment when an impasse was being reached in the relations between history and drama, when it was becoming impossible to use historical subjects. What can be conceded to Hebbel in this situation is that he produced a quite new kind of historical play; one which by the use of a particular subject suggests a broad philosophy of history. No one had done that before, and that is how Hebbel meets his problem. But the result, admirable according to the theory, has in practice the very serious defect analysed above.

The subsequent course of drama throws into relief the ambiguity of Hebbel's position. The historical drama did in fact disappear before very long. Ibsen clinches the development. His early historical dramas were the last to be seen in Europe, and they move us today less as great dramas than as great exercises in the "dramatic." He then took the logical way that Hebbel indicated with *Maria Magdalena* but drew back from; he abandoned the historical subject for the contemporary.

Hebbel's important plays are all tragedies, for tragedy is what he derived from his theory. It is the tragedy of men or women caught in the conflict of moralities, of men and women who, in advance of their time, are innocent according to the new rule, guilty under the old, and fall victims to conservative consciousness. They are the sacrifice of a time out of gear. One observes here the incipience of a kind of tragedy that is relative; for in each work the author sees things as tragic in relation to a particular pattern of conventions, to a social scheme, instead of a metaphysical one. And this is a defect which is shared by all subsequent "social" plays from Ibsen and Hauptmann onwards. What is really involved is a questioning of the very basis of the tragic. To begin to make tragedy relative is to begin eliminating it. The knowledge that "tragic" circumstances were fifty or a hundred years later no longer so neutralizes them. Each of Hebbel's "tragic" victims is in this position: Kandaules fighting a superstition that will vanish, Mariamne opposing Herod who will be defeated by Christ, Agnes a burgher child loved by a prince. What he really expresses through them is the pathos of historical prematureness; they are souls astray in time.

A defender of Hebbel might say that the particular circumstances in a play of his do not matter so much as the general idea which they illustrate: the dialectic of moral evolution that operates constantly in the background or foreground of social life, and the continuous "tragedy" it causes. It might even be claimed that Hebbel with the perspicacity of genius performed the brilliant feat of adapting tragedy to a new consciousness of history, just as he had found a new form of historical drama. There is, however, too much of the theoretical in such a tribute—in dealing with Hebbel you are always being driven towards theory—whilst criticism is still faced with the problem of the work of art and the effect it makes out of its own resources. Each separate work of Hebbel is impaired by the historical or moral rationalization that is implicit in its origin, a part of its actual inspiration. Each fails to be a particular compelling tragedy in itself. But what we do notice is that each reflects a vaguely tragic feeling that is associated for Hebbel with his central idea; taken all together they flow from a tragic "Stimmung" of the author. This phenomenon was to be repeated, for the same can be said of Ibsen and Hauptmann; it is in fact the characteristic feature of drama allied to the social thought of the later nineteenth century.

We come here upon the reason why *Maria Magdalena* makes a more powerful impact as a tragedy than any other of the author's works. The issue, it is true, is a stern and rigid moral code that is capable of supersession; but what Klara has to fight above all is the power of character in her father that supports the code. It is an irrational force far more terrible than the code itself; one, moreover, that we all know and are constantly having to meet. It is not morality but the moral fanaticism of Anton that dominates the work and makes the tragedy. In the succeeding plays Hebbel failed to capture again the kind of power that he shows in drawing Meister Anton's character. Herod, for instance, is simply a barbarous and cruel tyrant, swollen with conceit, his will nothing but caprice. He has a crude sort of force, but without any trait that makes him human. His love for Mariamne is not an exaggeration of tenderness but an extreme form of despotic brutality. Her personal position is in consequence sad, unlucky, pathetic; but the situation as a whole is not of a kind to compare with what we find in the great tragedies.

A crucial point for criticism in regard to Hebbel's plays is that they move on two planes at once. There is the view of history which we have been discussing and which Hebbel always puts first in importance. And there is a violent conflict between man and woman which actually provides the substance of the tense situations of each play. It is possible that many people read and enjoy Hebbel's works from this point of view alone. Certain it is that Hebbel draws from this source an intensity of life that was not in any way to be derived from a theory about history, however grandiose. Such immediate vitality as the plays have lies here.

His profound absorption in the psychology of women is in its origin quite independent of his historical visions. He repeatedly links the two; but it is impossible to demonstrate a real, an inevitable connection. His first play, *Judith*, is a striking index of this fact. It is a heroic chapter from Bible history, reduced to the level of human psychology. The story handed down is of an action of completely impersonal significance: Judith's mission to liberate the Jews. Hebbel probes into this for a personal conflict. Rejecting the heroic religious atmosphere, he endeavours to show what purely human motives might impel Judith to her deed. He shows a Judith who sets out to slay Holofernes for the sake of her people but in his presence she loves him as the first hero of the time. Yielding to him therefore, she loses her innocence as the mere instrument of Jehovah's purpose; she is personally involved, and is thrown into moral confusion. The sense of defilement turns her love into hatred, and it is this that gives her the desire and the strength to slay Holofernes.

This first play lacks completely the historical meditativeness of its successors; but the latter are almost all made of the same psychological substance. There is no mistaking the kinship of the tortured relations between Judith and Holofernes with those between Golo and Genoveva, Herod and Mariamne, Kandaules and Rhodope; and the woman is always the real focus of the piece. *Judith* shows us where Hebbel first found a material for drama; and the following plays show us that he continues to draw on this source for the body of his plays even though his historical theory alters the whole foundation of his creative purpose. He forcibly combines an intellectual perception with a purely psychological interest; a drama of historical dialectic with one of erotic relations. From the one comes the grandiosity of his idea, which we perceive when the play is over; above all, when we look at all the plays together. From the other derives the instinctive life of the play as it unfolds before us. It is an uneasy partnership, betraying a lack of organic unity.

Hebbel's ideas about drama and the moral conflicts of the age show him standing on a frontier of dramatic history. It is apparent, too, from the character of his verse and the way he uses it. He is the last of the dramatic poets who followed Schiller; the first to show a subject-matter connected with nineteenth-century social thought and treated in prose. He himself alternates between the two media. *Herodes und Mariamne* and *Gyges und sein Ring*, his two weightiest essays on the historical theme peculiar to himself, are in verse. *Maria Magdalena*, which is most directly connected with future developments of drama, is in prose.

His verse marks the long persistence of the Weimar tradition, and also its decline. A single passage from *Herodes und Mariamne* will show Hebbel's limitations:

MARIAMNE. Du sprichst umsonst! Du hast in mir die Menschheit
Geschändet, meinen Schmerz muss jeder teilen,
Der Mensch ist wie ich selbst, er braucht mir nicht
Verwandt, er braucht nicht Weib zu sein wie ich.

Als du durch heimlich-stillen Mord den Bruder
Mir raubtest, konnten die nur mit mir weinen,
Die Brüder haben, alle andern mochten
Noch trocknen Auges auf die Seite treten
Und mir ihr Mitleid weigern. Doch ein Leben
Hat jedermann und keiner will das Leben
Sich nehmen lassen, als von Gott allein,
Der es gegeben hat! Solch einen Frevel
Verdammt das ganze menschliche Geschlecht,
Verdammt das Schicksal, das ihn zwar beginnen,
Doch nicht gelingen liess, verdammst du selbst!
Und wenn der Mensch in mir so tief durch dich
Gekränkt ist, sprich, was soll das Weib empfinden,
Wie steh' ich jetzt zu dir und du zu mir? [1]

This quite representative extract is very flat for a crucial passage. Words and phrasing are commonplace, the sentences awkward and harsh, the lines and the sense without rhythmic unity; the last line alone is impressive, and yet even its simplicity is clumsy. A statement so relevant to the central idea called for better verse. One thinks of Goethe's naturalness and variety, his rhythm and euphony, his imagery; of the dramatic force and clarity, the rhetorical idealism of Schiller; of Grillparzer's melodiousness, his delicate emotional tones, his spontaneous grace. What characteristic quality in Hebbel could declare him a poet at their side? No writer communicates so much the sense of a forced poetic effort, of versifying to fulfil a laudable literary intention. He was still near enough—so one tries to explain it—to his great predecessors

[1] MARIAMNE. You speak in vain. You have dishonoured me, and with me all humanity; all who are human like myself, man or woman, known or unknown, will share my pain. When you robbed me of my brother with murderous stealth, only those could weep with me who have brothers of their own, the rest could stand aside with dry eyes and withhold their pity. But every man calls life his own, and no one will give up his life except to God who gave it. The whole human race condemns this crime; fate itself that allowed its inception and hindered its success condemns it; you yourself condemn it! And if humanity in myself suffers so deeply the shame you inflict, tell me, what shall a woman feel; how do we stand now, I with you, and you with me?

to wish not to abandon lightly a form they had made so splendid; and for his spacious historical idea he needed a dignity unobtainable through prose. His verse is that of a writer whose ambition is greater than his equipment.

The prose of *Maria Magdalena*, however, is incomparably more vital than his verse:

KLARA. Und wenn Karl doch freigesprochen wird? Wenn die Juwelen sich wiederfinden?

MEISTER ANTON. Dann würd' ich einen Advokaten annehmen und mein letztes Hemd daransetzen, um zu erfahren, ob der Bürgermeister den Sohn eines ehrlichen Mannes mit Recht ins Gefängnis warf oder nicht. Wär' es, so würd' ich mich beugen, denn was jedem widerfahren kann, das muss auch ich mir gefallen lassen, und musste ich es zu meinem Unglück auch tausendmal teurer bezahlen als andere, es war ein Schicksal, und wenn Gott mich schlägt, so falte ich die Hände und spreche: Herr, du weisst warum! Wär' es aber nicht, hätte der Mann mit der goldenen Kette um den Hals sich übereilt, weil er an nichts dachte, als daran, dass der Kaufmann, der die Juwelen vermisst, sein Schwager ist, so würde sich es finden, ob das Gesetzbuch ein Loch hat, und ob der König, der wohl weiss, dass er seinen Untertanen ihre Treu' und ihren Gehorsam mit Gerechtigkeit bezahlen muss, und der dem geringsten unter ihnen gewiss am wenigsten etwas schuldig bleiben will, dies Loch ungestopft liesse. Aber das sind unnütze Reden! Der Junge wird sowenig rein aus diesem Prozess hervorgehen, wie deine Mutter lebendig aus ihrer Gruft. Von dem kommt mir nun und mimmer ein Trost, darum vergiss du nicht, was du mir schuldig bist, halte du deinen Schwur, damit ich den meinigen nicht zu halten brauche! (*Er geht, kehrt aber wieder um.*) Ich komme heut' abend erst spät zu Hause, ich gehe zu dem alten Holzhändler ins Gebirge. Das ist der einzige Mann, der mir noch wie sonst in die Augen sieht, weil er noch nicht von meiner Schande weiss. Er ist taub, keiner kann ihm was erzählen, ohne sich heiser zu schreien, und auch dann hört er alles verkehrt, darum erfährt er nichts! [2]

[2] KLARA. And what if Karl is acquitted after all? Supposing the jewels are found? MEISTER ANTON. In that case I would go to a lawyer, and if it cost me my last penny I would find out whether the mayor was right or

Trying to maintain ambitiously a verse tradition that was spent, Hebbel was inferior; his finger on the pulse of something new, he was good.

For the point of view here adopted, the critical problems raised by Hebbel's work are important because they are symptomatic of a crisis in the history of drama, and of the relations between drama and poetry. Through his predecessors Goethe and Schiller he is linked with the great Renaissance tradition, doing his best to maintain "universality" and poetry. But he is a contemporary of Dumas fils and a forerunner of Ibsen in his social phase. He looks both ways, and much that is unsatisfactory in his work might be explained by a desire to make the best of both worlds. He has sensed the direction of a quite new movement of drama; but his development after *Maria Magdalena* seems to indicate that he drew back from the full consequences. He had the mentality, moreover, that takes less interest in particular contemporary "conditions" than in general ideas; and, rightly or wrongly, he proceeded on the belief that the general idea was more

wrong to throw the son of an honest man into prison. If he was in the right, I would bow my head, because what can happen to any man I must put up with as well. And if I had the bad luck to have to pay for it a thousand times more dearly than others, it would be the hand of fate; if God strikes me, I fold my hands and say: O Lord, Thou knowest what Thou doest! But if he were wrong, if the fellow with the gold chain round his neck rushed into it with only one thought in his head, that the tradesman whose jewels are missing is his brother-in-law, then we'll see if the law hasn't a leak somewhere, we'll see whether the King, who well knows he must return justice for the loyalty and obedience of his subjects, and who I'm sure wants to be indebted least of all to the humblest of them, will leave the leak as it is. But what's the use of all this talk! The boy has as much chance of leaving the courts innocent as your mother of leaving her grave alive again. He'll never bring any comfort to me, so don't you forget what you owe me, you keep your oath, so that I don't need to keep mine! (*He is going, but turns back.*) I shan't be back till late, tonight; I'm going to the old timber-dealer in the hills. He's the only man who still looks me in the eyes as he used to, because he knows nothing about my disgrace yet. He is deaf; nobody can tell him anything without shouting himself hoarse, and then he hears it all wrong, so he gets to know nothing.

conformable with the best poetic effect. His work is therefore for the most part a compromise between a traditional convention, the historical subject with "universal" implications, and a very precise reference to his own age and its problems. In analysing this result more closely we are always acutely aware that Hebbel's problem was drama's problem; he happens to be the writer in whom the symptoms first appear, and in their sharpest outline. They are evident again in Ibsen, who proceeds, however, in the opposite direction to Hebbel. He starts off with history and general ideas, and the verse-form, and then turns to the problem play in prose. He is more successful in the sense that his moral attack, launched by a relentless intellect, is clear and powerful; and his plays have a consistency and unity that Hebbel's lack. He is not more successful, however, in poetic conception. He is in the same dilemma, and the symptom in his work is his snatching at the poetic by the use of symbols; they indicate less the presence than the absence of poetry. From Hebbel onwards the inspiration of drama and of poetry flowed in different channels. The poets of the time, from Théophile Gautier to Yeats, were in revolt against bourgeois and materialist values. On the other hand, social thought and the growing moral conflict of the bourgeois world offered to drama a subject of obvious theatrical effectiveness. But the price for this advantage was immersion in the bourgeois world, in analysis, and in prose; and that led away from the values the poets were seeking. It was also a price too high for a form in which style and poetry must be identical with dialogue. Hebbel's compromise is unsatisfactory. Yet in the midst of his failure he is still aware, and we are as we read him, of a great poetic ideal.

EFFECTS OF IBSEN

"Yes, Ibsen is ugly, common, hard, prosaic, bottomlessly bourgeois—and with his distinction so far *in*, as it were, so behind doors and beyond vestibules, that one is excusable for not pushing one's way to it. And yet of his art he's a master—and I feel in him, to the pitch of almost intolerable boredom, the presence and the insistence of life. On the other hand, his mastery, so bare and lean as it is, wouldn't count nearly as much in any medium in which the genus was otherwise represented. In *our* sandy desert even this translated octopus (excuse my comparison of habitats!!) sits alone, and isn't kept in his place by relativity." So Henry James wrote in a letter to Julian Sturgis in 1893. Ibsen was one of those artists whose work divides people from the first between admiration and hostility. Not every artist does this; it is not the infallible criterion of originality; and it is not simply a question of a novel inspiration that is in advance of its time and comes later to be accepted. People of mature and discriminating taste, not ignoramuses, separated into opposite camps over Ibsen's work or, like James, felt there was a doubt. It was precisely what happened with another great artist of the nineteenth century, Wagner, especially in regard to his *Tristan and Isolde*. In such cases it is true that in one sense time and familiarity soften the harshness of the first opposition, and the work establishes some sort of position for itself. But it is also true that the division of opinion, the fundamental disunity of esthetic judgement in connection with it, continues; often in the form of a conflict in one's own mind. Nietzsche and Thomas Mann perpetually succumb to the "diabolical" fascination of *Tristan and Isolde* and perpetually cast suspicion on the sources of it and that part of themselves that responds. When this happens it is because the work itself does in fact raise some profound issue concerning the nature of art and its relation to human values.

The "social problem" plays of Ibsen are in this category and their influence will be the main topic of this essay. The difficulty of approaching Ibsen, of getting to like and admire him and acquire a fair judgement about him, is due to the disproportionate importance of the social plays. They are only a part, and a relatively small one, of his work; but they are the part that made him a European force. Younger people cannot feel directly, as older critics still do, what Ibsen's challenge meant and the powerful impact he made on European opinion. A proper understanding of it can now only be obtained by a laborious process of reconstruction which involves, I think, a very willing exercise of the historical sense and also reading a great deal of the writing about him that was contemporaneous with productions of his works. For the appreciation of his work as a whole, and for our present approach to him, the separation of the social plays from the rest has been unfortunate to a degree, although it was inevitable. Can it be said that appreciation of Ibsen's work as a whole has even begun?

There were in Ibsen from his earliest period two very powerful forces, one an overriding passion for Truth, or perhaps rather Truthfulness, and the other an exceptional sense of dramatic situation based on the interplay of character.

By temperament he was an idealist, but an idealist with only one ideal. If others evade facts and become romantics of illusion, Ibsen faced them and became a romantic of Truthfulness. Many have seen what they term a new "classicism" in his drama, meaning apparently an objective picture of life and a strict analytical technique. But below the surface, and below the superficial German romanticism of the early plays, it may be that Ibsen is profoundly romantic, possibly in fact the great belated dramatist of the whole romantic movement. He used drama to present in impersonal terms a personal struggle. Like Racine and Shakespeare he was a master of an extensive range of character-portrayal; but whilst their protagonists give a cumulative picture of Man, his repeat the picture of the rebel against society, in the sense of integrity against hypocrisy, of independence against cowardice, of spiritual vitality against deadening convention. He creates a myth of the Truthful Man, and the settings of his plays show a drama of symbolism to drive home the ideal. The vistas of fiords and hills, the boats going to sea, the steeples and mountain-tops, all there to lure his principal characters away from society, into the free distance, out into a clean natural air, upwards to a rarefied unpolluted sphere, to a solitude for strong spirits—they all mark the freedom that is consonant with the achievement of his personal ideal; and they mark too, often tragically, the separation of the ideal from life.

The other powerful force in Ibsen's work was, as indicated above, his interest in dramatic situation. The excitement of a rapidly moving plot and of dynamic events is a part of his drama, and it is invariably built up on the basis of a compact and full picture of character and life. But its most original aspect is an extraordinary sense of precipitated crisis. His situations portray the quintessence of crisis and they seem to have been shaped under the compulsion of an acute emotional response to the utmost concentration of conflict and tension. In Ibsen this has the character of a primary poetic experience. It is an immediate feeling for the dramatic as a phenomenon of life, a sensuous, almost mystical contact with the very concept of drama, over and above the particular details of persons and events in which it appears. He is always a master of such detail; but in play after play he transcends it and communicates a sense at once emotional and abstract of the pure dramatic. He is the supreme artist of the dramatic, and his name has become a byword wherever the essentials of the art are inquired into.

Of the two strains thus singled out for brief comment, the latter is directly evident in the historical plays, *The Vikings at Helgeland* and *The Pretenders*, where it has the field to itself. In most of the other plays there is a varying interfusion of the two. In earlier ones, *Love's Comedy*, for instance, or *Brand*, the sense of personal statement is predominant. In the period that opens with *Pillars of Society*, the two are in powerful conjunction, though the idealism of truth takes the impersonal form of a remorseless analysis of motives and "ideals" in social living. The last phase, from *Hedda Gabler* on (though *Rosmersholm* is on the borderline), shows a similar combination, but the personal theme is now transformed into a study of the perversion of originality, of the canker in the rose, of the character in whom the creative free independent truthful spirit is distorted by the demonic, assailing from within or without: Hedda, Solnes, Borkman, Rubek.

In his histories, in the plays with an almost autobiographical element, *Brand* and *Peer Gynt*, in the plays of the last period, Ibsen is most dramatic and most poetic at one and the same time. The work of the middle period is highly dramatic, but the creative imagination is subordinated to a critical analysis in the cause of truthfulness. It is the work that had an immense influence on the drama in Europe.

Under the impact of this subject-matter that had a pronounced contemporary interest, a controversial value, and a social application, writing and production in the English theatre burst into a great efflorescence; and yet the movement failed to produce great dramatic literature. That is the remarkable fact and the critical problem. The novelty and immediacy of the subject-matter, and the conscientious temper of the new writers, were clearly notable and warranted all the excitement they caused. It seemed that the theatre was being liberated effectively from stereotyped entertainment, and art rescued from the estheticism of the "nineties"; and if vitality is to be measured by these things and by extent of production and imitation, the new type of play would certainly claim that quality. It attained a front position for itself. For a generation the most widely accepted notion of what a good play should be was a thoughtful play for thoughtful people. From Shaw and Granville-Barker, through eminent and minor playwrights alike, and not forgetting the timely assistance of reflective rational Euripides, who was played as often as anyone else, down to a recent work like *Thunder Rock*, in which we see a last low ebbing of the tide, the type has dominated the stage and criticism.

Looking back now on the period that produced *The Voysey Inheritance* and *Candida*, *Loyalties* and *The Skin Game*, *Outward Bound* and *A Bill of Divorcement*, *Young Woodley* and *The Vortex*, *Robert's Wife* and *Dangerous Corner*, it is incredible that it should ever have been called "great." All these plays are competent, some of them excellent; all of them are representative plays of ideas, all successes of their time. Nevertheless they can attract now but little critical interest. The phenomenon as a whole, however, the drama *à thèse* reigning for thirty years in a royal state, is of acute interest for a critical history of drama. The type had been known before, but it had never held sway over the very conception of drama, never been glorified into the pattern of dramatic perfection. It is worth while trying to find an explanation of how a period went wrong when it did so on such a grand scale.

The explantaion lies in Ibsen's middle phase, the principal feature of which is that a very powerful dramatic technique coincided with a general wave of social thinking. Ibsen, as we have recalled, treated a variety of subjects in the course of his career. His great range is part of his distinction; the social subject was only one of his lines. But it was of the highest significance that he turned to social subjects in a period when his technical powers had reached their height. Advanced thought in Europe was already directed to social problems; the drama was debilitated; the combination in Ibsen of social interest and great new dramatic power produced the impressive new creation. The "serious" drama, the didactic social problem play was launched under the best conceivable auspices. It was a tremendous success; it was blindly imitated; it possessed the theatre.

Ibsen's work was, and to some extent still is, extraordinarily deceptive because of the sheer technical skill he displayed. But he had developed it in the plays he wrote previously to his social dramas. And those gave him much more genuine poetry than the dialectic of beliefs or the critical diagnosis of social habits could. Through this development, however, he obtained a degree of craftsmanship that enabled him to handle the social subject-matter in a masterly fashion. He gives every appearance of having met successfully the difficulties caused by its casuistic inspiration. Applying the massive technique that he had nourished from quite different roots, he made the new drama plausible as art. To this piece of virtuosity was due the new movement in the theatre, the establishment of a new ideal of what drama should be and do.

The detached spectator of today can more easily see how the social problem plays of Ibsen do not compare for artistic unity with his earlier or later work. One can readily admit admiration of the degree to which Ibsen, hammering—according to the familiar picture—at his material, working out in months of contemplation at his desk the "biographies" of his characters, does impose some kind of unity; admiration of the way in which he fits to his moral analysis persons and situations conceived so skilfully that they have a great semblance of naturalness, sometimes even of inevitability. But can one forget for long the double purpose? The dissociation between a "message" and an artistic apparatus is not to be hidden. The curtains of the first two acts of *Ghosts*—Mrs. Alving catching sight of Oswald kissing the maid, and the burning of the orphanage—are examples of a kind of artificiality that comes from moral and social difficulties being focused by the manipulation of persons and circumstances.

Archer, the pure critic, saw the defect in this hybrid between opinion and art, and he seems to have regretted that what he rightly considered Ibsen's best work was not his most influential. Pure criticism was not the forte of the play-writing disciples, or of the "serious" public that acclaimed them. They seem not to have had the acuteness that enabled Archer to see where Ibsen was great as a social critic and where he was great as an artist. They seem to have overestimated the usefulness of the real conflict their drama took for its subject, arguing perhaps in this way: Conflict is the essence of drama, therefore conflict transferred to the stage will be good drama. Only such a misjudgement explains the anxiety to imitate Ibsen. Their imitations, however, show how much in him was due to the special use of an extraordinary equipment; how the type of social problem play launched by Ibsen, having its real origin in ratiocination and debate, rests on false foundations by comparison with the tradition of drama and with Ibsen's own best. Without the master's personal force, his conscience and his challenge, this type shows up at once as an aberration. Ibsen himself abandoned it.

It was through Ibsen, therefore, that the idea of drama was standardized as an analysis of conflicting social and moral attitudes cast in the mould of tragedy or near-tragedy. The essentially practical inspiration of such a drama—the changing of manners and institutions—induced the highest respect for "realism." Analysis found its usefulness enhanced in proportion as it grew more and more *exact*, more and more photographic. Liberal truthfulness to life was the soul of the diagnosis. The very impulse of this drama eliminates the poetic imagination. The master himself tells us that in his social dramas he had to get more "prosaic," closer to "reality"; we believe him, he knew what he was about. His imitators, whilst they had no need of making any such sacrificial descent, spread themselves in the prosaic realism that dried up poetry and style at the roots. It was a boast of the time, pardonable enough in relation to stock theatrical entertainment, that drama had achieved its "intellectual freedom." The price paid for this distinction was its poetic life.

Thus Ibsen's liberation of drama was not, when we consider the results in England, so advantageous or so unquestionable as many have held. A very powerful writer had a very wrong influence.

It is to the credit of this body of drama that it was undoubtedly contemporary in spirit, even though it often was so in an obvious if not superficial way. To ignore the romantic and pseudo-poetic and try to discover new foundations in a social theme relevant to the life of the day was a sign of vitality. But it was only one half of the task of art.

The artistic failure of the social problem drama makes one ponder its relation to the art for art's sake movement to which in its early stages it was consciously opposed. The new dramatists accused the esthetes of sterility because they were remote from life. The artists might very well reverse the accusation and say that the playwrights might have contact with life but were remote from art. It is amusing to reflect at this distance that in one sense the esthetes come out of it rather better, since they at any rate didn't pretend, although they could be good at pretending, to have a great social message for whole communities, whereas the people with the social interest did pretend to have art. Every art has objective conditions which might be modified by new subject-matter but cannot be ignored; hence tradition. The writers of social problem drama, misled by the example of one phase of Ibsen's work, did neglect the conditions of art, and so produced a body of work that may have been influential and successful at a certain level, but lacked poetic distinction.

SHAW

For the spectator who is interested in poetry and drama and theatre in their interfusion Shaw is embarrassing. "The poet in Shaw was still-born," writes Eliot. We have all felt again and again an extraordinary deflation as soon as the curtain has fallen. The agility and wit of Shaw's social criticism holds his plays together and casts his spell into the auditorium. The plays do not live as plays beyond the fall of the curtain. As they draw to a close they do not give the feeling of a building being completed; the forces which propel them are indeed bent all the other way, towards demolition. These works do not, after their emergence in time, solidify, as the great dramas do, into a shape for the memory; they leave us without the retrospective vision of form achieved. And yet Shaw cannot be thought out of the theatre by a theory of drama and poetry. It is not so much that he has simply conquered the stage and made it serve his own purposes; he has also, in spite of our reservations, served some of *its* purposes; of that there is as little doubt as of the fact that he has not served all its purposes or its greatest, as Jonson and Molière did.

There is a certain quality of calculation in Shaw's approach to comedy. It may be a wonderful calculation, of which the pleasantest thing to say would be that it is the "instinct of his genius." He has never hidden the fact that he is at heart an evangelist; and he has thirsted for more souls than the pamphlet—"his" form if ever there was one—could procure. He tried the novel. But he is essentially a man of ideas, of agile intellectual criticisms, and the novel, with all its apparatus of description and report, is a bore to him. Moreover, the audience of the novel is the individual; and the object of Shaw's criticism is society. In the theatre he catches three large groups who together make up the whole of mankind except its eccentrics: those interested in entertainment, those interested in ideas, and those interested in art. He catches them, moreover, in their social agglomeration and cohesiveness—his address is to society, and there it is assembled before the stage.

Having turned to the theatre, it was undoubtedly a stroke of personal genius to choose comedy for his form in the conditions obtaining in the theatre and intellectual life generally at the turn of this century. Comedy carries didacticism with a better grace than other kinds of drama. If there are to be ideas and debate in plays, then they offend the intellectual nature of comedy less than the emotional nature of tragedy or "serious" drama. There are reasons for Shaw's eminence that have less to do with the theatre proper than with his person and his ideas; but here is a reason for his eminence that springs from the very conditions of theatre and drama at that time. In an age of "problem plays" comedy, as a form, even though it does lose something, loses less than other forms. Shaw therefore appears as the culmination of an epoch that was opened by Ibsen (Dumas fils was of course a harbinger). He may dominate in part by qualities that would have given him eminence outside the theatre; but he also dominates on grounds of drama alone, in the age in which he wrote. It is a culmination, viewed broadly, of three things: social thought, its application in the theatre, and Shaw's own conviction, aggressively held, that art should always be parable. His work is the *best* effort of all the drama that was inspired by social criticism. It is even superior to Ibsen's, where Ibsen's implications are social.

The novelty of Shaw's comedy called forth inevitably protagonists and antagonists, and it has been defended mainly as a comedy of ideas in contrast to one of manners or situation. That battle is won. We know now that in Shaw's "pamphlets in dramatic form" we have to watch the drama of ideas, of which persons and events are the diagrammatic illustration.

As an iconographer, he has with consistent conscientiousness always given us both the theory and the example, the thought and the illustration, the preface and the play. And no doubt the only proper way of judging his work finally is one that takes account of the unity of preface and play.

This is the tribute that Shaw wrests from us; compelling us to ask the question that has always been asked since romantic criticism taught us to put it: what unique quality of personal experience is he endeavouring to convey?—before we judge his work. Yet matters do not end with this romantic interest in personal messages, and unique ways of stating them. Shaw claims to be an artist and he works in a well-recognized form; and so it is fitting to recall that art may depend on artists, but artists also depend on art. Artists may revolt; they also submit. Forms—lyric, dramatic, narrative—admit of extensive variation, they are developed and modified. Yet they are not without a certain constancy of character, and impose, sometimes when we are least aware of it, an authority of their own which is above the single worker. Shaw does not escape. One could write a lot about him with the merest reference to comedy as an art with traditions. But he did not create his form out of the void; he selected it from amongst others for his use, and he owes something to it. Again, at the moment he entered the theatre, drama had been given a powerful direction by Ibsen; he owes something to this too. In the relation between what he owes and what he gives criticism discovers something both about drama and about Shaw.

Within the limits of the art of comedy he has displayed a striking originality in two principal directions; first in the point of view he adopts for his critical attack, and secondly in his adaptation of comedy to the naturalist technique.

Regarding the first point, Shaw conforms to tradition in the sense that you must have a fixed point from which to work, to launch your criticism. In Molière, for instance, the established position is generally interpreted as the rule of the golden mean of reason. Shaw is also devoted to reason. But whilst Molière takes his fixed point from the general experience of men as rational and social beings, Shaw takes his from a rational philosophy of his own. Hence he inverts the usual method. Instead of isolating the unreasonable character, he isolates the reasonable one. Molière gives us a series of characters who offend our idea of rational behaviour: Harpagon, Alceste, Arnolphe, Argan, Tartuffe are examples. Shaw, on the other hand, gives us a series that illustrates his own idea of rational behaviour: Dudgeon, Caesar, Tanner, Dubedat, Undershaft, Shotover, Magnus, Joan, and so on—all characters with a head, with their eye on the point, piercing illusions and grasping reality.

The difference is accounted for by a difference of interest. Molière—and we can say Jonson too—feeding on the thought of the Renaissance, was interested in a conception of man; Shaw, under the influence of the thought of the late nineteenth century, in a conception of society. His main attack being on society, his transformation of traditional comic method is brilliant. Taking an unconventional character, a person with the gift of insight and freedom, he impinges it upon a group of conventional social animals, and the impact reveals at every turn stock notions and reactions, prejudices and dishonesties, in short the illusionary, the unreal, the irrational. Molière exposes one character in turn; Shaw the social herd, all together. And these characters of his are most certainly dramatic conceptions, because they create, by being what they are, startling situations.

It is not necessary to dwell on the remarkable efficacy of

this transformation for Shaw's purpose. It shows itself all of a piece with the man, his temperament, his challenge, his message. We accept it as an instrument supremely adapted to its use, and acknowledge the immense talent that could make such an adaptation of a comedic method. But this is the point where, if we cannot detract from the personal genius of Shaw, we can arraign the artist, for the cunning of the method cannot cover the inadequacy of the result, when we apply the standards set by the highest imaginative comedy. Molière's Harpagon and Alceste, Jonson's Volpone and Sir Epicure Mammon, are imaginative creations. You cannot agree or disagree with them; in their simplicity and ideality they *are*. They have an existence and a permanence that are unassailable; and they are, moreover, centres from which moral energy radiates with an operation that cannot be limited by the fall of a curtain. Shaw's principals are not products of this kind of imaginative power. At the most it can be said that his series has a certain force and solidity because each member of it is a reflection of Shaw's own intelligence, and their effect is cumulative. The core of each one of them lies in their critical penetration, a quality of their creator. It is their only real vitality. They are without the vitality of instinct that makes a total living creature and on which the characters of Molière are based. For this reason we remember less what they are than how they talked; and every time we disagree with their opinions they lose some of their power. Each one of Molière's great creations is an image of a human folly, and he leaves us a whole gallery of them. Shaw gives us but one image: of the critical mind acting as a solvent. There is a point outside the drama where the two authors meet, on the ground of philosophy and practical wisdom, or the effort towards it. It would be difficult to decide which is the greater intellect. But it is easy to judge Molière the greater artist, because he gives us forms, against which Shaw can only put a *perpetuum mobile* of critical comment.

The second point about the mutual relations between Shaw's personal aim and the dramatic form concerns the realist convention in which he works. His comedy flowing from his criticism of society, he needs for his purposes the ordinary social milieu, with the sort of crisis that arises from typical bourgeois circumstances. In this milieu he lets his unconventional characters challenge the creatures of habit by word and action, and the rest follows. His material is that of all bourgeois drama since the middle of the nineteenth century, more particularly since Ibsen. One of the things he admired most in the latter was the way he made his audience feel that what they saw on the stage was what went on in their own homes. The direct attack is of the essence of Shaw's intention. His method in fact is to give us a comic version of Ibsen's principal theme, the rebel against society, the true man against the false. Ibsen being swayed on the whole by the Germanic seriousness, by some deep-seated emotional need for tragic crisis, his subjects and treatments were generally the reverse of comic. Here and there, however, he explores this latter vein, and *An Enemy of the People* appears as the embryo of Shaw's comic method. In developing his work from this position Shaw achieves a remarkable feat. For in the first place comedy and wit introduce a compensating element of imagination into the lamentably prosaic waste of bourgeois realist drama; Shaw avoids the mistake of other imitators of Ibsen. And in the second place he liberates comedy from the cruder forms of its long-accustomed artificialities and tricks—the disguises, the eavesdroppings, the mistaken identities, the stock characters and so on. They have been the properties of comedy since Plautus and were made necessary by the demands for concentration and sustained liveliness of situation in the theatre. Having found another source of vivacious movement in his unflagging raillery, Shaw dispenses with the traditional tricks as the main tools of construction, and uses the "realistic" social scheme. Not that he foregoes altogether the prerogative of comedy in the matter of fantastic incident and improbable dénouement. In fact he gains here another advantage over the "serious" social problem dramatist, because he can treat more cavalierly the difficulty of contriving a probable end as well as a probable situation. He may use far-fetched incidents and dénouements, but they are not the part of his material that really counts. For example, the arrival from the air of Percival and Lina Shchepanowska in *Misalliance* is quite fantastic, and so is Lina herself in the circumstances of the play; but the basic situation had become a commonplace one of contemporary social life. The incident in itself adds superficially to the entertainment; no writer of stage comedy, not even Molière, can afford to neglect any source of amusement, and Shaw has the good sense to be as small on occasion as his greatest predecessor. But even so, the real Shavian comedy is independent of the bit of fantasy; for it follows when we see the impact of Lina, an original character, a free woman and true to herself, on the convention-drenched people around her.

These are the two principal features of Shaw's work which make a mutual relationship between him and his form clear. Our first impulse is to say: this is not comedy as it ought to be. Our second is to justify it as the proper mode for Shaw's idea. With our third impulse we look more closely at work that seems to owe no obligation except to its own law, its own subject-matter, and we discover that it does owe something to its genre, to its predecessors, to pre-existent authorities. It illustrates a continuity, not a break. Shaw adheres first to the principle that comedy must have a fixed vantage-point, though he transforms it to suit his own purpose. He retains, too, the prerogatives and tricks of comedy, without, however, the necessity of being chained to them. He also keeps to stock types for comic purposes, but his new social philosophy gives him a new set of types. Even in incidentals he can follow well-worn grooves of the art; the Straker-Tanner relationship in *Man and Superman* rests on the conventional master-valet set-up, given a completely new vitality from the new social background. And his second great obligation is to the dramatic developments that immediately preceded him and in which he was caught up. He uses the natural probable situation of bourgeois life, public or domestic, that focuses a problem of social behaviour. And he acknowledges the debt by originality of treatment; that is, he gives us what no one else gave and Ibsen had only hinted at, comedy.

CHEKHOV

CHEKHOV's is a refined art; and it is extraordinary how so delicate a writer has succeeded in the dramatic form which in the past had depended on much more elaborate and tense plots, events of greater violence, and more impetuous dynamic characters. He pays the scantest deference to the rules, satisfied if in a general way he can suggest movement and climax. It would be wrong to say that nothing happens; something is going on all the time, often something very large, from the psychological point of view. Uncle Vanya has lost his zest for life and we watch him lose the love that might have brought it back. A young poet sees his work coldly received by a successful writer, and the girl he loves seduced and abandoned by him. Three sisters struggle without success to find a meaning in their narrow provincial lives. A woman sees her property sold, her class and the values it stands for ousted by a new life that seems vulgar to her, and she is helpless. But such psychological happenings, as portrayed by Chekhov, are given a movement so slow that it almost negates itself and becomes simply a continuing condition. The fallings in love, the hysterics and nervous crises are symptomatic recurrences within this condition, marking the routine, not breaking it. Hence the remarkable effect of such violent actions as Chekhov does on occasion use—Treplev's suicide, Tusenbach's duel, Vanya's attempt at murder: they may, technically speaking, fulfil the function of a climax, bringing down a curtain, but they are felt to be less significant and less terrible than the state they interrupt. Such incidents in plays are usually the final catastrophe of a tense development and their effect is to inspire terror, and also to bring release through closing the development. Chekhov divests them of this kind of dramatic significance; they pass, and the condition remains. Their dramatic function is less in themselves than in throwing into relief a picture of permanent frustration.

Konstantin Treplev, in *The Sea Gull*, trying with some agony to find a style of writing, makes the following remark: "I come more and more to the conviction that it is not a question of new and old forms, but that what matters is that a man should write without thinking about forms at all, write because it springs freely from his soul." It is an observation that might safely be taken in reference to Chekhov himself, because its very generality is so characteristic of him. His treatment of life is to a great extent independent of definite forms sanctified by traditions; it is one reason why he is original. It doesn't matter to him very much whether he writes stories or plays; he handles each with a minimum regard for any theory or ideal of form. What he had to say he was able to transmit with a fair neglect of the architectonic element in the technique of the larger forms, of drama and nouvelle. The "form" in his work derives to a large extent from the visionary impression, the representative and epitomizing trait of character or speech or incident, and the smaller units of rhythm. He is, for instance, a master of the movement of impulsive feeling; when irritation and temper break out, or sentiment and love, or pity and sympathy, often in rapid alternation. He is at his finest in the creation of atmosphere and mood, particularly moods of suffering, frustration, and of aspiring thought. He is also expert at sketching in, with varying degrees of caricature, the drollery of subsidiary characters, small-scale line and colour that is less than foreground but more than background, delicate but vivid pieces in the pattern.

His extreme fineness of touch and subtle feeling for tone enable him to portray with a very acute sense of life characters who in many ways lack life, certainly energy and robustness. The people of *Uncle Vanya*, *Three Sisters* and *The Cherry Orchard* are some of them intelligent, some stupid, but nearly all ineffective; and those who are or have been active, like Astrov the hard-working doctor with his plans of work and development, or Olga the headmistress, feel that their strength is giving out and that failure is written over their struggle. Such vitality as is left to all these characters goes to feed a single slender flame of consciousness: that they are parched. Their souls have no energy, but they are still souls; their characters no aggressiveness, but they are still characters; their persons no will, but they are still aware of will, they know it is needed and they haven't got it. All the art of Chekhov, withdrawn from larger outline and concentrated on tremulous detail, goes into making this lifelessness, this paralysis vibrate.

He shows his people in their detachment from affairs. Their daily occupations, activities, and professional duties, where they have any, are not overlooked, but they are important only as the broad foundation of monotonous or purposeless or hopeless disillusioned lives. The immediate contrast is Ibsen's world, its people immersed in their businesses, their undertakings, their newspapers, their mayors and councils, their clergymen; the public arena, the social cross-currents providing a great stir of character and plot. Chekhov, in selecting his scene, virtually eliminates the buzz of practical affairs, and presenting his persons without the rigidities of the "well-made" play, he allows us to observe them within the inner chamber of their character. He descends upon them in their leisure moments and discovers them not as servants of a job or a duty or a purpose, propelled by practical reason or animal egoism, but as men and women who, however paralysed their wills may be, are conscious of their souls and seem to wait on some great transfiguration. Setting them free in this way from all conventional appearances of work and economic struggle, Chekhov shows an essence of spiritual character. Whatever their intellectual degree or moral rank, whether they are odd, or bored, or aspiring, or fluttered, or empty, or intensely suffering, these people are laid bare in their spiritual condition. It is upon this end that the artistic process of selection is bent. If a form is the emergence of an idea in terms of sensibility, Chekhov gets his form by isolating in the lives of his men and women the moments in which they are spiritually awake, when they hear a profound inner voice that detaches them from a lifeless material world and plunges them into a vital sensitiveness; when they suddenly become alive to questions, mysteries, meanings and the lack of them; when they become, in feeling, revolutionary. They hear echoes of worlds transcending their own, where love is requited, where there is less suffering, where men are happy; and they then have their characteristic impulse to do something to make the dream real, an impulse which in an odd sort of way is part of the dream itself. With such a purpose in his selection Chekhov is really testing his people for the nature of their souls. When they fail the test outright he satirizes them; those who are sensitive at all he portrays at the least with tenderness and at the most with tragic pathos, as in the case of the three sisters.

But to leave it at that does not do full justice to Chekhov's idea. For through his people he is testing life itself. In seeking, as we have suggested, the moment of pure spiritual awareness, he is raising in his own mind, in that of his characters, and in that of the spectator, the great problem of what constitutes the quality of life outside an immediate practical purpose. He is using a touchstone which is essentially that of all philosophy and all art; and he has made his dramatic form itself shape the question. How far are the values of life inseparable from the technique of living—from the economic struggle, the job to be done, the social adjustment, the simple moral victories? Is there a value that transcends all this, and what is it? What is the spirit, when it is free?

The magnitude of the question puts it amongst those that are valuable simply by being stated; they are signs at once of human endeavour and limitation. The curious mixture in Chekhov's plays of an ardent will to the remedy of "work"—they are always crying: We must work, we must work!—and of a deadening sense of futility is symptomatic. It indicates the mystery that lies between the knowledge that we can never attain perfection and the feeling that we must try.

Chekhov has always caused astonishment by the subtlety with which he seems to capture the movement of life itself; and one of the problems for criticism is to reconcile this extraordinary touch for "reality" with the poetic effect that is one of the most certain impressions left by his work. It is possible that his apparent closeness to reality, the very success of his nervous and sensitive response, has the paradoxical consequence of obscuring the extreme degree of selection that he exercises over his material; and his selection is all directed to revealing a delicate idealism of the inner life. Chekhov is a great idealist. His sentiment, his humour, his satire, his humanity, his form, his poetry, spring from this central fact.

By virtue of his idealism he has created people with all the potentiality of happiness and goodness. There are no rogues in Chekhov. There is no wickedness of character; the evil lies in the great shadow cast over life generally. Trigorin, who is the cause of unhappiness, is selfish, not vicious. Doctor Lvov, in the early play *Ivanov,* is a foolish meddler, but far from being bad he is a misguided idealist. Lopahin, the man who buys the Cherry Orchard, has the best intentions. To get a variety that makes his picture more natural, Chekhov uses absurd and ludicrous types in place of wilful or malevolent ones. His caricature, especially in *Three Sisters* where it is most mordant, is the vehicle of some of the bitterness that is in his picture. But it throws into relief the yearning of the central characters. There are, moreover, some very odd scenes. It is queer that people should sit talking about the future happiness of mankind whilst the town burns just outside. Yet in the midst of frustration, even of comicality, these people are for the most part noble. Flat, bored, sterile, helpless, they never cease to break out in impulses towards universal love, happiness, the ideal, beauty in nature and beauty in man. Irina's words "my soul is like a wonderful piano of which the key has been lost" might apply to most of Chekhov's characters; it epitomizes the whole scene of life. The pathos of *The Sea Gull*—a curious meditation on artistic types—lies in the fate of the two young sincere artists, Konstantin and Nina, at the hands of the showy successful ones, Madame Treplev, vain and self-centred, and Trigorin, the minor writer with a large established following. Something fragile—the spirit, an idealism, a yearning for poetry—is broken. There are no "moral problems" in Chekhov's work as in Ibsen and his disciples; but everywhere there is moral aspiration. The satirical strokes are an indirect indication of it, and the criss-cross of unrequited loves, and also the expressive scenes of departure and farewell, the sadness of parting being the sadness of desolation and exclusion.

In the series of full-length plays Chekhov wrote there is a growing insistence on the social implications of the life he portrays. In the first, *Ivanov,* one notices little of it. The theme is clearly introduced in *The Sea Gull,* however; it is more unmistakable in *Uncle Vanya*, reaches a clearer form still in *Three Sisters*, until finally in *The Cherry Orchard*, where a self-made man buys the orchard from a hereditary proprietor in order to cut it down and develop the site for weekend bungalows, the action is provided by the supersession of one social class through another.

The social theme was a predominant one in the work of many of Chekhov's contemporaries. He is distinguished by an absolute subordination of particulars to a generalized "Stimmung," the character of which derives from the idealism we have spoken of. Hauptmann's social dramas, for instance, depend entirely on an interest, stimulated by philanthropy, in localized conditions: what it looks like amongst peasants who ruin themselves and their offspring by their craving for alcohol, or amongst impoverished weavers exploited and crushed by capitalist enterprise. Ibsen's social plays depend on localized problems; they show the domestic or the public crisis that arises where there is a conflict between moral beliefs held with conviction or obstinacy. Both these things—the portrayal of "conditions" and the analysis of particular principles—are absent in Chekhov. We sense certain currents in the atmosphere of his plays: criticism of a given state of society, the intellectual apprehension of the causes of change and the necessity of it, all the knowledge of what is going on, the moral judgement passed by a new idea upon an old order. But argument is avoided, whilst suffering is portrayed. Ideas are skilfully diffused amongst his characters and made to appear as part of the texture of life itself:

VERSHININ. Yes. They will forget us. Such is our fate, there is no help for it. What seems to us serious, significant, very important, will one day be forgotten or will seem unimportant (*a pause*). And it's curious that we can't possibly tell what exactly will be considered great and important, and what will seem paltry and ridiculous. Did not the discoveries of Copernicus or Columbus, let us say, seem useless and ridiculous at first, while the nonsensical writings of some wiseacre seemed true? And it may be that our present life, which we accept so readily, will in time seem queer, uncomfortable, not sensible, not clean enough, perhaps even sinful. . . .

TUSENBACH. Who knows? Perhaps our age will be called a great one and remembered with respect. Now we have no torture-chamber, no executions, no invasions, but at the same time how much unhappiness there is!

SOLYONY (*in a high-pitched voice*). Chook, chook, chook. . . . It's bread and meat to the baron to talk about ideas.

TUSENBACH. Vassily Vassilyevitch, I ask you to let me alone . . . (*moves to another seat*). It gets boring, at last.

SOLYONY (*in a high-pitched voice*). Chook, chook, chook. . . .

TUSENBACH (*to* VERSHININ). The unhappiness which one observes now—there is so much of it—does indicate, however, that society has reached a certain moral level. . . .

VERSHININ. Yes, yes, of course.

TCHEBUTYKIN. You said just now, baron, that our age will be called great; but people are small all the same . . . (*gets up*). Look how small I am.

Chekhov's picture is of a social situation as a whole, but he builds it up from innumerable traits in individuals, and to this is due its intense liveliness. The subject, in one of its important aspects, is the temper of a society, but within this main idea there is presented a world of everyday human hopes and ambitions, loves and hatreds, despairs and sadness, follies and discretions. The picture is indeed so generalized as to render any narrow interpretation of its social meaning false; there is a suggestion of timelessness that makes it a picture simply of human life. Of this *Three Sisters* is the best example, and if universality is the final test, it would rank as his greatest play. *The Cherry Orchard*, on the other hand, having the more explicit social theme, is the more skilful demonstration of how that theme can be treated imaginatively; it is more than illustration of social conditions or of an abstract idea, it is poetic statement.

The question arises in this connection as to how far Chekhov's plays reflect an actual state of society capable of documentation, or how far they express simply his own feelings about life. How true is his world to a historical reality, or how true is it simply to his personal view?

The answer would seem to be that he found a point where a dominant note of social life corresponded to a dominant feeling of his own; and his feeling was determined by a visionary sense of impending social change. He is able in consequence to be veracious about himself and about society at one and the same time. Because his own feeling is clear to his imagination the state of society is clear as well. His observation showed him the symptoms and his idealism gave him the right interpretation. This accounts for the extraordinary blend in his work of an objective picture and a lyrical emotion that comes from his own idealism. It is a blend that is extremely rare in drama, which as a form tends to the highest degree of impersonal statement, seen at its greatest depth and range in Shakespeare. At the hands of an idealist–Schiller is a very good example–the objective picture usually suffers through distortion or exaggeration.

If from the first production of *Ivanov* in 1887 at Moscow Chekhov's technique startled people by its strangeness, it was only what is constantly happening in the world of art. The form was new for a new subject. The characteristic playwriting method of the later nineteenth century is completely rejected. The "well-made" plot is replaced by "scenes" (Chekhov actually calls *Uncle Vanya* "scenes from country life") showing a group of associated persons and a sequence of incidents which are less important as part of a plot than as symptoms of a social condition and an emotional frame of mind. This "condition," to which almost everyone is subject, even servants, is more than a framework for a drama; it is itself the drama. A spiritual malaise experienced by society as a whole is shown as a crisis. Chekhov's form has the great virtue of being an organic one. He achieves with it a fineness of fibre that makes him unique amongst his contemporaries in the theatre. Here is some of the subtlety and poetry that

Henry James wanted to find a place for in drama; some of the delicate spiritual response to life that Yeats missed so keenly in "realist" plays. Chekhov's artistic vitality lies in his bold adjustment of dramatic form to his vision and to the modern situation.

His limitation in handling the medium is that he only secures a part of what it can give. He was sceptical of rules and theories, and when he achieves as much as he does by following his inspiration, adverse criticism can easily appear niggling. Yet it would be over-zealous to take the success of his free manner as a plain demonstration that traditional experience in the form is valueless. There are some writers whose subject exactly suits the genius of the form or medium they choose, and others whom the absence of this correspondence forces to rely on a free use or variation of one of the traditional forms. Drama raises this problem more acutely than the novel because its conditions are so much stricter. What we must recognize is that a larger form like drama gives pleasure in itself, a pleasure which the audience shares with the dramatist and which is even present where the literary value is low. The "drama," the "dramatic," is at least part of the object in view, and the form naturally seeks an intensity of pleasure in proportion to the concentration of its means. All the greatest dramatists knew this, whatever their subject, their philosophy, their analysis of life; and at their best they combine a maximum of the ethos of their form with a maximum of life in their subject. Chekhov belongs to the group that adopt a form less for its own sake than for their own particular uses. His independence led him to neglect the utmost concentration of means, and he did not attain the degree of surrender to the dramatic medium that we observe in Racine, in Ibsen, or in Molière. In consequence he got less, from the form as such, in return. His originality is of the kind that is to a large extent achieved in spite of the authority of the medium. Shakespeare and Racine are great artists in a double sense: not only because a vision of life unfolds itself, but because their medium, too, unfolds its character and its powers. Chekhov is a great artist in the simple sense that he found the right terms for the presentation of his particular idea.

SYNGE

IN THE first years of this century, when Shaw had preached people into taking up Ibsen and when he and Granville-Barker and others were pioneering the drama along its new paths distinguished by service and utility in causes other than those of poetry, Yeats was telling Synge in Paris to go and "express a life that had never been expressed." Synge left the centre of *fin de siècle* culture and took himself off to the Aran Islands in a canvas canoe. Turning his back on the social problem, on French esthetes and symbolists, he discovered in his western world an original subject-matter and language. Out of these he formed an opus so fascinating that it made him an object of great adulation.

Synge writes in the pithy Preface to *The Tinker's Wedding:*

The drama is made serious—in the French sense of the word—not by the degree in which it is taken up with problems that are serious in themselves, but by the degree in which it gives the nourishment, not very easy to define, on which our imaginations live. We should not go to the theatre as we go to a chemist's, or a dram-shop, but as we go to a dinner, where the food we need is taken with pleasure and excitement. This was nearly always so in Spain and England and France when the drama was at its richest—the infancy and decay of drama tend to be didactic—but in these days the playhouse is too often stocked with the drugs of many seedy problems, or with the absinthe or vermouth of the last musical comedy.

The drama, like the symphony, does not teach or prove anything. Analysts with their problems, and teachers with their systems, are soon as old-fashioned as the pharmacopoeia of Galen—look at Ibsen and the Germans—but the best plays of Ben Jonson and Molière can no more go out of fashion than the blackberries on the hedges.

By following this line Synge has got a remarkable reward. He is judged the greatest dramatist of his time in the English and Irish theatre. If we except Yeats he is certainly unique amongst his contemporaries for poetic sensibility, although he wrote in prose. His work appears as a challenge to the stultifying realism of the debating drama. But we might venture now, without losing our admiration for the rarity of his achievement, to see that his star does shine so very brightly because there were so few others in the sky; and to see, too, that it is a luminary wholly attached to a nineteenth, not a twentieth century orbit.

Synge is a very romantic writer. At the beginning of *The Aran Islands* he writes: "It gave me a moment of exquisite satisfaction to find myself moving away from civilization in this rude canvas canoe of a model that has served primitive races since men first went on the sea." Synge's flight heightens itself into a symbol of his nostalgia for the primitive—in manners, nature, in speech and scene and music, in the whole setting of life and culture. He is of the latest progeny of Rousseau and Herder: a romantic the more exquisite for being tardy. Herder in particular would have liked these near-to-nature people of Synge's, the sentiment of forest and solitude in *Deirdre,* a folk-speech of natural poetic power, an aura of musical ideality around the cabins of these mean though lively persons, the source of story and character in folk-lore and legend. There are in the dialogue innumerable touches of a lyrical response to nature:

"I stood a while outside wondering would I have a right to pass on or to walk in and see you, Pegeen Mike, and I could hear the cows breathing and sighing in the stillness of the air, and not a step moving any place from this gate to the bridge" (Shawn). "For what good is a bit of a farm with cows on it, and sheep on the back hills, when you do be sitting looking out from a door the like of that door, and seeing nothing but the mists rolling down the bog, and the mists again and they rolling up the bog, and hearing nothing but the wind crying out in the bits of broken trees were left from the great storm, and the streams roaring with the rain" (Nora, in *The Shadow of the Glen*).

This is a romantic feeling for nature impinging on genre pictures of peasant low life. Mingling a lyrical mood with his realism, Synge throws a halo around an everyday of primitive, sordid, almost brutish motive. It helps not only to endow his people with a higher human interest, but it is essentially the inspiration on which his characters may be said to live, rather than on the interest of character itself. Synge has been much praised for his character-drawing; it is a point on which his genius has been quite inappropriately compared to Shakespeare's. His characters certainly have liveliness—especially when compared with the artificially constructed persons of the contemporary problem dramatists. But they are the merest sketches; their vividness is that of suggestive line-drawings. Of his two most developed characters, Christy Mahon and Deirdre, the former subsists entirely on a single comic idea and the latter on a single lyrical aspiration. And though it is true that Synge's vision of their life has universal aspects, it cannot be claimed for his work as a whole that it enlarges our view of human character and behaviour, as the work of the Elizabethans, the Restoration dramatists, of Racine and Grillparzer and Ibsen does.

Synge's lyricism has been noted as a secondary concomitant of his drama, rather than as the dominant note. Yet Padraic Colum reports that Synge told him "all his work was subjective," "it all came out of moods of his own life. *Riders to the Sea* had come out of the feeling that old age was coming upon him—he was not forty at the time—and that death was making approach." This is more applicable still to *Deirdre of the Sorrows,* of which we remember Yeats writes in *Dramatis Personae:* "On the first night the thought that it was Synge's reverie over death, his own death, made all poignant." Clearly, beneath an apparently impersonal picture presented by Synge there is an inspiration that is profoundly lyrical.

Through this mood the legendary material of Deirdre, for instance, received an expression of a quite personal kind. The legend is an ordinary drama of concupiscence, jealousy and power. It is made stately by various traits: the traditional dignity and elevation of the characters and their remoteness in time, and the conventional but eternal image of a queenly beauty that is resplendent and destructive. The motives that Synge ascribes to Deirdre, however, make the play into an expression of a romantic aspiration for love and beauty; for the beauty of nature and the beauty of woman, the beauty of youth and infinite passion.

For Synge's reverie over death is a reverie over love, and the romanticism of the work lies not least in the conjunction. Death appears in the long tragic shadows Synge skilfully throws from the very beginning of his drama: the continually repeated suggestion that Deirdre's fate is pre-ordained, unalterable. It is a knowledge which is woven into her character, occasioning an infinite sadness and also a sublime courage. Deirdre nurses her destiny, she is strangely constant to it, even whilst eluding it for a long period. But the lyricism of the work is clarified above all when Synge shows how Fergus comes with the summons to return to Emain and be reconciled with Conchubar. For the motive that Synge gives to Deirdre in resolving upon the return is a great fear of weariness in love, a fear that her love or Naisi's might decline and be defiled. It is a psychological twist which, I think, weakens the tragedy; for when Deirdre wishes for death from *this* motive it is no longer a catastrophe. But what breaks to some extent the point of the tragedy reveals the lyrical import of the play. It gives us an intense expression of romantic love, related in its feeling to Wagner's *Tristan and Isolde*. Naisi and Deirdre have lived seven years for love alone, detached from men, absorbed by their self-sufficient passion. The time appears to Deirdre as a heavenly perfection, and to prolong it to eternity she cuts off her life.

The measure of the lyrical element in Synge's drama can be taken by comparing it with Yeats's treatment of the legend. If we consider the essentials of the inspiration before the appearances, Yeats's must be judged the more dramatic work. It is more so technically because he concentrates the action upon the return to Emain and the final betrayal. But it is not only a matter of skilful construction: Yeats has preserved the "story" of Deirdre in a purer form. It is a genuine retelling for the sake of its universal truth of an old tale that can never be told and heard too often; and the lyrical genius of the poet supports the dramatic presentation. Synge on the other hand has saturated the traditional subject with a nostalgia for undying passion—which passes at the crucial moment into nostalgia for death for the sake of the passion; and in this case the dramatic genius supports the lyrical purport.

Riders to the Sea, too, expresses a mood, but it is not subjective in the sense in which *Deirdre of the Sorrows* is; the lack of personal feeling makes it by comparison an impersonal tragedy. Its lyricism lies elsewhere: in its way of presenting a natural atmosphere, its elemental sense of sky and landscape and sea and storm.

The action of the play is extraordinarily simple. An islander goes over the sea in defiance of the storm and the efforts of the women to hold him back; and he is drowned at once. But this action is presented as one that is constantly recurring. It is the threat under which the islanders live. In these circumstances its simplicity gives it grandeur. For the most remarkable thing about this work is the degree of tragic intensity Synge achieves whilst working on so very small a canvas. One is reminded of the way in which Maupassant achieves in some of his briefest tales an astonishing compression of force, an effect that gives him a stature far above that of the ordinary "short-story writer." In a similar way Synge's effect quite transcends the miniature scale on which he is working.

The tragic intensity achieved in this play has often caused writers to compare Synge with Shakespeare and Sophocles. Such enthusiastic comparison is bound to be a little unfortunate because one is too sharply reminded of differences. As a tragedy *Riders to the Sea* is without doubt remarkable in the way it presents unpretentious heroism opposing Sea and Tempest that hang like Fate over men's lives. But it has nothing whatever of the complexity of the tragic processes in human life that we find handled and mastered by the greatest writers. *Riders to the Sea* is a fine piece of tragic art precisely because it does *not* compare with *Oedipus Rex* or the tragedies of Shakespeare. It is elemental, but also bare and excessively simple. Its great power lies in its creation of atmosphere. This certainly has its dramatic force, as the scenes on the heath in *Lear* have. In Shakespeare, however, those scenes are but an immense background to an immense human complication and suffering. In *Riders to the Sea* the tragic sense emanates entirely from elemental nature. Its effect of impersonality is due to the dramatic form; its inspiration is largely lyrical.

The exotic appeal of Synge's work can scarcely be exaggerated; and it is another aspect of his romantic and lyrical character. I think there can be no doubt that Synge himself experienced the language and life he found in the Aran Islands as something rare and strange, beautiful because it was unsophisticated, remote, elemental. It awoke the artist in him, as Paris had not been able to do, because he was a romantic. And in this Synge is the pure artist, without any admixture of the political intentions that have always to be reckoned with in Yeats and other adherents of the Celtic renaissance. Yeats it was who sent Synge out to the West, helping a genius to find his line, but also making a démarche in the political cause of Irish nationalism. It is clear that Synge was independent of causes; an unpolitical artist, whatever use others made of his work once it was done. His pleasure in observing his primitives and in savouring their musical and picturesque language was from any point of view but the artistic irresponsible and non-commital. The storm about *The Playboy of the Western World* arose because there were many Irishmen who could not emulate such detachment.

As far as the Anglo-Saxons are concerned, I think Max Beerbohm came nearest to the truth when he stressed the exotic as the source of our greatest pleasure in Synge. It is, however, a judgement that has been obscured by more frequent tributes to his pure dramatic genius. No one would deny his natural sense of drama and theatre, his powers in comedy and tragedy. If he were without them his more personal charms would be thin and vapid perhaps. But he did not possess those powers in an astonishing degree, and they alone certainly do not make the Synge to whom we are endeared. They are the excellent soil above which the rare bloom raises its head. Synge's greatest distinction, the thing that gives our acquaintance with him its particular flavour, is his wonderful language, which pleases us not as a heightened form of the language we ourselves use, but as a picturesque deviation from it. Two things support each other; the setting of Irish character, atmosphere and speech is itself exotically attractive, and it is made more so, pointedly so, by Synge's exquisite and subtle handling of the imaginative peasant language he discovered in the West.

This view, with its emphasis on the pleasure we get from unfamiliar forms of life and language, runs counter to a simple appraisal of Synge's style as a great creation. It is "poetic" only within certain well-defined limits. It is very closely related to folk art and suffers from the same disadvantages. The "folk" imagination is spontaneous and beautiful as far as it goes; it does not always go very far. The simplicity and freshness and immediacy, the innocent and natural tones of folk art are not enough for mature phases of art. The influence of folk-song in German poetry, for instance, was beneficial in some ways, equally harmful, however, in others, for the reversion to its forms in the romantic era—after Goethe had outgrown them—retarded for nearly a century the development of new and more varied forms. Synge's language, for all its delicate modelling, loses in the long run by its limitation as folk-speech. In his slender production it suffices to express a rather narrow range of peasant character and simple feeling. Its style is all on the surface. It has not that expressiveness of great dramatic poetry that lies in its profound relevance to the underlying pattern of our own lives. Such language might be gorgeously metaphorical, as in Shakespeare, it might be eloquent, precise, intense, as in Racine, but it is anything but unfamiliar. Using the elements of our own language it completes and illuminates what we experience in an obtuse way. Judged by this proper standard, Synge's style is severely restricted. Where purer effects of dramatic poetry are required, as in *Deirdre of the Sorrows*—the one play whose subject-matter lies outside the range of his original discovery—his language in some passages even fails outright. Its picturesque or homely remoteness, so much a concomitant of its "poetic" appearance, obstructs the true effect of dramatic poetry. It diverts the attention to the surface instead of holding it upon the situation.

How much the idiom in itself has to do with Synge's art emerges from *The Playboy of the Western World*. The direct sensuous consciousness of a patently picturesque speech and way of thinking is the inspiration of this play; and the point gains in importance when we consider that this is his most ambitious work. The basis of the comic here is a delicate and capricious mockery at the very idea of fine language, closely related as it is to fine ideas. Synge plays in this comedy with his own discovery. Through his mock-hero Christy Mahon he allows his instrument to elaborate its most splendid ornaments. Some have been so entranced as to take it at its high face-value as sheer poetry. Yet it is the most precise exaggeration, a distillation of his own speech-material conceived in a vein of irony. Christy Mahon is a wonder to the people of Mayo and he talks himself into a wonder for his own imagination. Their reactions are focused in him. The figurative phrases that pour from his lips are his own beautiful amplification of *their* response to the lad he was, of their fancy for the stupendous notion that he had killed his da. Fine words argue the fine idea, the alert imagination. The people who play up Christy are quick in esthetic reaction; for the sake of a fine story they instantly suspend their moral judgement. Synge brings them back to it:

PEGEEN. I'll say a strange man is a marvel, with his mighty talk; but what's a squabble in your backyard, and the blow of a loy, have taught me that there's a great gap between a gallous story and a dirty deed.

It has been pointed out how Synge got the germ of this drama from an old man on Inismaan. His use of what he was told points in the direction of the argument we are putting forward. He heard how a man who killed his father was protected by the islanders until he could be got off to America. Synge comments: "This impulse to protect the criminal is universal in the West. It seems partly due to the association between justice and the hated English jurisdiction, but more directly to the primitive feeling of these people, who are never criminals yet always capable of crime, that a man will not do wrong unless he is under the influence of a passion which is as irresponsible as a storm on the sea. If a man has killed his father, and is already sick and broken with remorse, they can see no reason why he should be dragged away and killed by the law.

"Such a man, they say, will be quiet all the rest of his life, and if you suggest that punishment is needed as an example, they ask, 'Would anyone kill his father if he was able to help it?' " Synge has so transformed both the initial situation and the attitude of his characters to the doer and his deed that it is almost true to say he owes nothing to the story told him. He discards the event in its original form and substitutes a pure fantasy. And he quite changes the motives of the peasants. The mixed impulse of pity and charity and obscure reverence which made them help the unfortunate parricide he replaces by a gay and reckless love of a marvel told, and told marvellously.

Surprisingly enough, Synge's delicate self-mockery in *The Playboy of the Western World* leads us back in a roundabout way to the esthetic cults of the *fin de siècle*. Synge immersed himself in a local material—men with sharp profiles, living a hard and lowly life—and he has given such a vivid picture of them, that his physical severance from Paris and its artistic currents seems at first sight to have its complete counterpart in his work. But looking below the surface of these *genre* pictures, of this apparently impersonal drama, one discovers other things. This comedy is not directed only against the people of Mayo, but against Synge himself; against the artist and his dangerous love of fine words. It is at once the fullest display—conscious display—of his most distinguishing gift, and an ironic commentary on it. The love of fine words for their own sake, symbolized in Christy Mahon at its intensest though in a comic inversion, is a form of the search for something ethereal and esthetically refined, some musical quintessence. It was very original of Synge to discover this in a milieu that was in no way artificial or recherché or ultrasophisticated; nevertheless it shows him in closer relation to some literary tendencies of the atmosphere he deserted than is generally supposed. Synge's work is most praised amongst that of his contemporaries for its imaginative quality; it is less often noticed that his most ambitious work has for its very theme the imagination, the fine idea and the fine word. From this point of view it is one of those works, often of dubious inspiration, in which the artist takes art and artists for his subject. It is, however, wonderfully disguised; and the disguise—the comedy and the irony—gives it its quality.

Viewing Synge in some of the ways I have tried to indicate means modifying a little our more excessive tributes of praise. His real achievement is that he went his own way when almost everyone else in drama was fanatically social and "contemporary," and he found something akin to the poetic in an out-of-the-way place, with the result that his work goes on living with the life of imaginative creations when those who imagined themselves to be so intensely "alive" are dead. And yet from the point of view of the English drama during his lifetime and since, his work has been singularly unhelpful, however fine the figure he makes. For the drama wanted at that time two things: a poetic form and a contemporary consciousness. The latter it had in a crude way; the former it lacked entirely. With Synge the position was reversed. His consciousness was nineteenth-century and romantic; he looked backward, not forward. On the other hand, he had, within the limits we have indicated, a style, but one that was quite useless for the English drama, its basis being a speech of extremely local and ambiguously English character. He is therefore without influence on English dramatists. The misfortune in this is that our drama sadly needed a poetic influence from somewhere. It required an innovator to start a movement towards dramatic poetry; as Ibsen had started one in subject-matter, the culmination of which in England was

Shaw. If Synge's work had been wholly English instead of tantalizingly ambiguous it might at least have provided such an initial impulse. As it is, from the point of view of the tasks of drama in England, Synge might almost as well never have existed. He is a fortuitous visitor in our sky, shedding a brilliant and decorative lustre but no fertilizing warmth.

YEATS

YEATS's dramatic creation is not bulky, yet its variety is considerable enough to make a general characterization difficult. *The Pot of Broth* and *The Resurrection; The Cat and the Moon* and *Deirdre; The Player Queen* and *The Words upon the Window-pane;* they present striking contrasts of subject and method.

Many strains and impulses operated to produce complexity: a debt to French symbolist poets that has little to do with drama, though it influences profoundly the verbal texture of the plays . . . a devotion to political causes which led Yeats to seek a correlation between the highest in literature and the highest in national life . . . feelings and essences of the spirit that are often prolongations of romantic sensibility . . . a pure enthusiasm for dramatic statement, for "showing events" as well as telling about them, as a high form of poetic art . . . the discovery of what was cognate in his own imagination with that of the Irish countryman . . . immersion in a theatre movement that sprang from and rebounded upon a true community or at least the ideal of one . . . the endeavour to find dramatic expression for trance-images and spiritisms that derived from a personal mysticism . . . the revulsion against "realism" on the stage, and the search for aristocratic style and sentiment, for "ancient technicalities," for truth and beauty . . . all these things influenced him separately or concurrently and almost every play is shaped by a different combination of them.

On the nature and technique of drama he has an admirable theoretical passage in *The Irish Dramatic Movement:*

> What attracts me to drama is that it is, in the most obvious way, what all the arts are upon a last analysis. A farce and a tragedy are alike in this, that they are a moment of intense life. An action is taken out of all other actions; it is reduced to its simplest form, or at any rate to as simple a form as it can be brought to without our losing the sense of its place in the world. The characters that are involved in it are freed from everything that is not a part of that action; and whether it is, as in the less important kinds of drama, a mere bodily activity, a hair-breadth escape or the like, or as it is in the more important kinds, an activity of the souls of the characters, it is an energy, an eddy of life purified from everything but itself. The dramatist must picture life in action, with an unpreoccupied mind, as the musician pictures her in sound and the sculptor in form.

This description could apply to any significant drama, even a very complex one, the greatest effort of art being to reduce complexity to simple statement. But if Shakespearean tragedy, for instance, is an illustration of the general import of the passage, Yeats's own plays illustrate it only on a narrower literal reading and on a smaller scale. He worked, moreover, to a formula that represents the technique of construction at its least complicated, however sound: suspense based on the principle that the most effective dramatic surprise is that which is half foreseen. A single, often loose, knot, untied with a single movement—such, for the most part, are his plays. But within this restricted framework he can be extremely dramatic, and *The Only Jealousy of Emer* or *At the Hawk's Well* show it quite as much as the more conventional *Deirdre* or *On Baile's Strand.*

A note of 1916 for *At the Hawk's Well,* written after many years of experience, shows that Yeats had laid his finger directly on one of the greatest difficulties:

> Shakespeare's art was public, now resounding and declamatory, now lyrical and subtle, but always public, because poetry was

a part of the general life of a people who had been trained by the Church to listen to difficult words, and who sang, instead of the songs of the music-halls, many songs that are still beautiful. A man who had sung "Barbara Allan" in his own house would not, as I have heard the gallery of the Lyceum Theatre, receive the love speeches of Juliet with an ironical chirruping. We must recognize the change as the painters did when, finding no longer palaces and churches to decorate, they made framed pictures to hang upon a wall. Whatever we lose in mass and in power we should recover in elegance and in subtlety. Our lyrical and our narrative poetry alike have used their freedom and have approached nearer, as Pater said all the arts would if they were able, to "the condition of music"; and if our modern poetical drama has failed, it is mainly because, always dominated by the example of Shakespeare, it would restore an irrevocable past.

But I think one might go further than this, for it is not only changed relations with the audience that cause embarrassment. Yeats from the beginning was struggling with other things besides Shakespeare's sterilizing domination, now in its third century; above all, as far as English theatre was concerned, with the lapse of all traditions of acted verse-drama, in association with new creation, over a very long period. He was contending, too, with his own subject, which was not easy to mould into a dramatic shape and for which there were no models to help him. And he had to compete with the main tendency of the time, "realism."

Elegance, subtlety, music. . . . Giving rein to his impulse to keep Shakespeare at the greatest possible distance, Yeats went, finally, to Japan for a model, to the aristocratic "Nō" stage. He had written a number of plays before he found this form; and in the Preface to *Plays in Prose and Verse* he says that *Four Plays for Dancers* are a different form of art, meaning no doubt that for their highly collaborative character the dancer, musician and sculptor are as important as the poet. But there are many indications that works like *The Shadowy Waters* tend towards this model that sets a seal on his searchings. He was to write plays later that in their turn receded from the model, like *The Resurrection;* but its presence is still felt.

It is largely the discarding of the logical plan and characterization, the twin supports of conventional playwriting, that makes Yeats's dramas so elusive to traditional expectations of the form, and provokes the criticism that they are undramatic. Drama had always depended on an action that took a natural form as it is observed in life. It seems almost to be a rudimentary condition of an art that is made up of impersonation, of presenting a picture of body and speech and behaviour. The logic of appearances; the close analytical plan with its explanation of relationships; the exposition of character and motive within a coherent moral order; the observance of time and space as they are accepted by common sense—all this is the foundation of Sophocles and Shakespeare, of Calderon and Corneille, of Molière and Congreve. And if a supernatural or dream world is presented, it is always a phenomenon having its place within the larger rational framework, as in *The Tempest.* Here, moreover, lies the common ground between drama in verse and drama in prose. *Deirdre* and *On Baile's Strand* are examples of it in Yeats.

The drama that was in vogue when Yeats was writing, the prose realism of Ibsen, Hauptmann and Galsworthy, reaches the extreme of dependence on natural logical appearances. Its critical purpose makes this inevitable, for it sets out to observe a "real" state of affairs and must achieve accuracy of diagnosis. To the extraversion of moralists and sociologists Yeats opposes in most of his plays a world inward and fanciful and spiritual; to their logic he opposes emotion; to their socially coherent plots his spiritually coherent visions. It is not only a question of "stylization," of beautiful verse and design, supported by formal elements of chorus and ballet, ennobling an action from life. "It would be a stirring adventure for a poet and an artist, working together, to create once more heroic or grotesque types that, keeping always an appropriate distance from life, would seem images of those profound emotions that exist only in solitude and in silence." The mask, the patterned screen, the formal accompaniments of drum, gong, zither, and flute, the dance figures of the performers, design in the speaking of verse, are powerful independent means of evoking emotion; Yeats uses them in combination to give "musical" depth, a field of reverberation, to the action and to the language, which in itself employs rhythm, sound and image with the same intention. An early play like *The Shadowy Waters* relies entirely on the resources of language. The *Plays for Dancers* show the technique in its full development. And the poet's effect flows finally from an imagery of emotion that is intense in proportion to the complex use of different media towards a single end.

The result of such an assembling and ordering of symbols is to add a function to action itself. Instead of treating a plot that illumines human relations in their moral aspect, Yeats makes action into another signature of "emotion." It is not an end in itself, flowing from and dependent on what we call "character," but it evokes instead the intimacies, ecstasies and anguish of the soul-life. In these subtle plays relations between men matter less than the submission of a soul to the all-enveloping spiritual mystery. The coherent action-sequence that illustrates essentially the *moral* nature of life gives place to a complex pattern communicating a spiritual insight. In this pattern action is sometimes, it is true, an element of the seen life of human relations; more often it is an element of the unseen life of the soul and of spiritual powers, presented in poetry through anthropomorphic images.

In the mingling of these elements of seen and unseen, of natural and supra-natural, of human and divine, "action" comes to have the force of symbol, and conversely symbol assumes sometimes the character of action. One of the most striking illustrations of this transposing of character and function is to be found in *The Cat and the Moon.* The framework of the play, beginning:

> The cat went here and there
> And the moon spun round like a top,
> And the nearest kin of the moon,
> The creeping cat, looked up.
> Black Minnaloushe stared at the moon,
> For, wander and wail as he would,
> The pure cold light in the sky
> Troubled his animal blood

describes a landscape and a relationship between cat and moon. The song appears to be mainly descriptive, but its impact is dramatic, and in a double way. For there is drama in the play of occult silent dialogue between the animal of nature and the cosmic moon; and when we remember also that the phases of the moon symbolized for Yeats the phases of the soul's life, we see that the song has a symbolical reference to the drama of the beggars and the saint, and that it thereby heightens the dramatic intensity of the whole work. Its structural use, opening and closing the play, with a middle section inserted in the dialogue, is only the outward sign of the deeper relevance. On the other hand, the *obvious* action of the lame and blind beggars starts off on the plane of everyday reality, of human relations, only to pass to miracle and finally to pure symbol for spiritual truths, pure "image of emotion."

In using action in this intricate and exceedingly free way Yeats has drawn on ordinary human life, on religious mystery, on folk-belief, on a mythical spirit-world, on a region of fairies and fantasies, on poetic legend, on occult spheres. The world he creates out of these various elements is not an "unreal" one, though it is very different from the world we are accustomed to find in drama. As a mental world that is relevant to our life it is real. The poet's means may often be those of fantasy, but his end is always to express something not at all fanciful or remote but exceedingly proximate: a mental, spiritual, emotional reality. *At the Hawk's Well*, for example, presents a feeling that is a substantial, gripping experience, it is "intense life"; only the object, the thing-to-be-attained is remote and elusive. Irrealities are symbols that evoke a reality.

The real fault in Yeats, I think, is not that his subject is unreal, uncorporeal, immaterial, but it lies in the *degree* to which he sometimes refines away the material world in too many directions at once. The effect is seen if we compare *The Cat and the Moon* with *The Dreaming of the Bones*. In the former, the figures of the beggars have a corporeal quality and their speech—in prose—the sound of earth, even though the action gradually attains to the miraculous and symbolic. But in the latter, occultness and "unreality" in the action is often matched by a dialogue that uses continuously images that are certainly sensuous but are chosen to express unsensuous things:

YOUNG MAN. My Grandam
Would have it they did penance everywhere;
Some lived through their old lives again.
STRANGER. In a dream;
And some for an old scruple must hang spitted
Upon the swaying tops of lofty trees;
Some are consumed in fire, some withered up
By hail and sleet out of the wintry North,
And some but live through their old lives again.
YOUNG MAN. Well, let them dream into what shape they please
And fill waste mountains with the invisible tumult
Of the fantastic conscience. I have no dread;
They cannot put me into jail or shoot me;
And seeing that their blood has returned to fields
They have grown red from drinking blood like mine,
They would not if they could betray.

At points like these the poet flies too much in the face of the conditions of a spoken form.

Another confusion arising from Yeats's very original handling of action gives rise to the criticism that his plays are more lyrical than dramatic. There is obviously a close relationship between the subject-matter of many of Yeats's plays and that of much lyric poetry. The emphasis on spirit and "emotions that exist only in solitude and in silence" serves also to differentiate these plays from others. The difficulty arises, of course, with the *Plays for Dancers; Deirdre*, *On Baile's Strand*, *The Pot of Broth*, and similar works, are straightforward. Yet even where Yeats is expressing "emotions," he is doing it by means of dramatic statement; there may be a lyrical way of doing it, but he has given us the dramatic way, and a refinement of method is not to be mistaken for a confusion of form. In all his plays there is a direction, a movement, a crisis, which alone is the instrument revealing the "emotion." *The Dreaming of the Bones* is one of the most delicate of his plays, one with the most attenuated action, one of which it would be easiest to say that it is undramatic; and I have just urged a criticism against a passage taken from it. Yet even this play is essentially dramatic in conception. Its emotion is the most fanatic Irish patriotism. But what gives definition to the emotion in all its intensity is an act; the refusal of the Young Man, in flight from the enemies of his country, to extend forgiveness to the tormented spirits of Dermot and Dervorgilla, the lovers who betrayed Ireland to the foreigner seven hundred years before. Little by little the spirits of the dead lovers unfold to the Young Man the picture of their long terrible penance, and as they do so the depths of history reveal the powers of a nation's vitality, converging upon the present moment and renewed by the implacable act of the young patriot. The figures in this play are one man and two ghosts; but the passions evoked are those of a whole nation of men and the life of centuries. The dramatic intensity of the climax lies in the perspectives it unfolds.

In Yeats three things work together which in creative writers had for a long time been antagonistic: spiritual, dramatic, and poetic values. He had a life to express, he was a poet, and he had an acute sense of the power of dramatic form. His plays, therefore, which have so distinct an originality that they might seem to call for a judgement only on their intrinsic value, have in fact a wider historical significance as well. For the continuity of drama and its connection with the main stream of poetic writing his work is much more important than that of either Synge or the "realists."

In technique he asserts in a new way the virtue of convention and formality, exploiting to the full the expressiveness of design in speech, movement, stage-setting and music. But his formal patterns are always appropriate; they are an extension of the convention of verse itself and fulfil the same function of enhancing expression, of making explicit the poet's theme and subject.

It was something that had vanished from European drama. One has to go back to Goethe's presentation of his *Iphigenie auf Tauris* to find a dramatic poet insisting on these values of formal style. Goethe's incomparable sense of form has been obscured by the readier interest of the nineteenth century for his philosophy. In acting, his rule was "erst schön, dann wahr," a principle derived from the interpretation of Greek art; and as long as we take this compressed phrase as a pithy precept and not as a complete esthetic there is no misunderstanding what Goethe meant. The drama in Yeats's time had cut itself off from such resources of form. Eliot was later to take up the question in his "Dialogue on Dramatic Poetry," where the ballet is admired as an artistic model for the reason that it compels the dancer to undergo a "training," an "askesis." He makes no reference to Yeats's experiments with

Plays for Dancers, but there is community of thought and effort.

In subject-matter Yeats broke new ground in attempting to adjust drama to the vital trends of artistic effort, which were towards the exploring of more and more complex and subtle mental worlds. He indicated that the content and expressiveness of the form could in fact be extended in a new direction. That he had emotion and vision of the kind that suit lyric poetry was under the circumstances more help than hindrance, because it freed him from the slavery of preconceptions. The picture of moral relations that we find in most drama was not his subject; so from the start he could search unhampered for the dramatic form of what was his subject. To have been more "dramatic" in the conventional sense would have done less for drama.

Yeats was not the first to use symbolism in drama, but he is distinguished by his deliberate, free, and intricate use of it, and by the way it openly dominates his "actions." There is a sense, of course, in which every drama is "symbolical." The events and characters in the plays of the Elizabethans or Corneille and Racine depend on the illusion of definite time and place, of particular circumstances which can have no exact repetition or counterpart. Their power to affect us, however, lies not in their local concreteness but in the symbolical truth of their psychology. Only Macbeth murdered Duncan; but Duncan is murdered every hour. When drama has this symbolical power it is said to be "universal." The characteristic of sixteenth and seventeenth century plays, however, is that drama has so identified itself with the life of emotion and action, of passion and will, that it seems to have nothing to do with symbols of any kind, but directly with "life."

Faust is the first great work in which the more complex experience of an individual is presented; experience that is religious and philosophical as well as passionate and moral, and which in consequence has more and more in it that belongs to a purely mental world. It is in *Faust*, therefore, that we find an extensive and patent resort to symbols and allegory as the only means of externalizing for this particular form an inward world, until Faust himself has become one great symbol of humanity; and again the "universality" of the work derives from this symbolism, now direct instead of indirect.

The organization of a play of Yeats is simply a further step in the same development; and seeing it in this way shows the vitality of Yeats's work, its vitality both of content and of form. He takes us perhaps to an extreme limit; but his way has its poetic inevitability. In Shakespeare and his contemporaries a world of spirit shapes itself upon a world of violent deeds because it was precisely this latter—the life of Renaissance man, a prince and adventurer, an amateur of love, ambition, power, intellectual and esthetic sensation—that raised the great moral and spiritual issues. The analysis of this life was the new subject for poetry prescribed by observation of the age. In this kind of work, therefore, spiritual experience flows from a real world of drama. In Yeats the new subject for observation is the life of the soul and spiritual powers, and so the progression is from inward to outward, unseen to seen, a sensuous world of drama shaping itself upon an ideal world of spirit. The novel can express mental experience directly. Drama is compelled to use symbolism, personification and myth. Yeats's use of a complex imagery of emotion was a vital method prescribed by the conditions of art and life in his time. The relative brevity of his plays depends on an acute judgement of what the method will stand.

Symbolism is here, too, the agency that makes explicit the universality of the theme. Only a superficial reading can take Yeats's plays as the expression of personal lyrical states of mind. These short plays are almost invariably concerned with great themes: Cathleen's sacrifice of self, Deirdre's affirmation of love, Forgael's nostalgia for a transcendent perfect joy,

Cuchulain seeking a god-like life at the Hawk's Well and drawing upon himself a blind human fate, Emer renouncing her love-dream so that her husband might live, the Lame Beggar preferring blessedness to cure, the sacrifice of charity to an overriding abstract passion in *The Dreaming of the Bones*, the rationalism of the Greek confronted and bewildered by religious mystery—we need not complete the list. Everywhere we find the permanent realities of the human situation, everywhere the recurrent drama of spiritual ecstasy and torment, brought to manifestation in some crisis.

HUGO VON HOFMANNSTHAL

WHEN he wrote the poems and lyrical dramas that first made him known in the early nineties, Hofmannsthal was associated with poets who were in violent reaction against materialism in philosophy and "naturalism" in art. There was only one shrine for poets to worship at: symbolism in Paris. In a poem written later, Stefan George sums up the general feeling:

Und in der heitren anmut stadt, der gärten
Wehmütigem reiz, bei nachtbestrahlten türmen
Verzauberten gewölbs umgab mich jugend
Im taumel aller dinge die mir teuer–
Da schirmten held und sänger das Geheimnis:
VILLIERS sich hoch genug für einen thron,
VERLAINE in fall und busse fromm und kindlich
Und für sein denkbild blutend: MALLARMÉ.

Mag traum und ferne uns als speise stärken–
Luft die wir atmen bringt nur der Lebendige.
So dank ich freunde euch die dort noch singen
Und väter die ich seit zur gruft geleitet . . .
Wie oft noch spät da ich schon grund gewonnen
In trüber heimat streitend und des sieges
Noch ungewiss, lieh neue kraft dies flüstern:
RETURNENT FRANC EN FRANCE DULCE TERRE.[1]

[1] And in the town of merry grace, in gardens
Of wistful charm, near nightly gleaming towers
With magic arches, youth was all about me
And swept away with all the things I cherish–
There bard and hero fended for the Secret:
VILLIERS who thought himself the peer of kings,

[Cont. on p. 130]

George's ideal at that time was a poetry of "Stimmung." It might be esoteric, or recherché, or exotic, so long as it was inward and cultured, and avoided contamination with raw life and the crude external social milieu of the time. It is obviously a narrow ideal of poetry. But its narrowness is explained by the deliberate purpose: to seek a musical intensity which is present to some degree in all art but was completely lost in the dry atmosphere of the sociological drama and novel. Pater's dictum about all the arts aspiring towards the condition of music sprang from a sensitive diagnosis of the artistic situation of that time. It throws light on the nature and unity of art in general, but the quality it singles out for the purpose is one that appealed particularly to a certain phase of poetic sensibility.

Hofmannsthal's early "lyric dramas" fit very well into this atmosphere from a broad point of view. But perhaps the element of "Stimmung" in them has been too easily accepted as a predominant characteristic that makes them more lyrical than dramatic. Though people were first startled above all by their lyric beauty, I think the present-day observer, viewing the whole development, sees something else that is even more exciting. Poetry is here linked with an instinct for drama. Hofmannsthal, like Yeats, had a craving for the theatre, for poetry in the theatre, and all his later development shows his devotion to it. Ultimately, therefore, he parts

[Cont. from p. 129]

VERLAINE in fall and shrift devout and childlike,
And bleeding for his concept, MALLARMÉ.

Though dream and distance give us strength and nurture—
Air that we breathe, the Living only proffer.
So friends who still are singing there, I thank you
And forebears that to graves I since have followed. . . .
As in my dreary land I strove, uncertain
Of victory, this whisper gave new vigors:
RETURNENT FRANC EN FRANCE DULCE TERRE.*

* Translation by Carol North Valhope and Ernst Morwitz from "Franken" in *Poems*, Stefan George, copyright 1943 by Pantheon Books, Inc., used by permission of the publishers.

company with many of his generation, particularly George, who included a social art like theatre in the world he rejected. Judgements of Hofmannsthal that are influenced by George break down on this point. Criticism has not to judge Hofmannsthal by his early lyricism alone, but to observe his progress towards a form of dramatic poetry. His problem was not dissimilar to that of Yeats, however much their work differed. As a young worker in verse he was bound to be influenced by the current ideals of verse, which were lyrical; and only maturity could give the dramatist in him the necessary independence. The lyricism of the early plays is due more to the general poetic atmosphere of the time than to a predominant lyrical inspiration of his own.

I do not propose to go to the other extreme and exaggerate the dramatic qualities of Hofmannsthal's early works. It is simplest, and good sense, to accept them as the mixed form that their title indicates. They have their lyrical mood and reflectiveness, and their central characters express feelings, and at length, that are often more meditative than dramatic.

Ein grosser Gott der Seele steht vor dir.
Wenn in der lauen Sommerabendfeier
Durch goldne Luft ein Blatt herabschwebt,
Hat dich mein Wehen angeschauert,
Das traumhaft un die reifen Dinge webt;
Wenn Überschwellen der Gefühle
Mit warmer Flut die Seele zitternd füllte,
Wenn sich im plötzlichen Durchzucken
Das Ungeheure als verwandt enthüllte,
Und du, hingebend dich im grossen Reigen,
Die Welt empfingest als dein eigen:
In jeder wahrhaft grossen Stunde,
Die schauern deine Erdenform gemacht,
Hab ich dich angerührt im Seelengrunde
Mit heiliger, geheimnisvoller Macht.[2]

[2] You see before you a great god of the soul. When in the mild restfulness of summer evenings a leaf fluttered through the golden air, my breath that hovers dreaming round the ripeness of things touched you with a

This passage from *Der Tor und der Tod* has its relevance in the scene between Claudio and Death, but the thought follows the imagination freely and transgresses dramatic necessity. On the other hand, the feelings and moods of these plays are not those of solitary contemplation. They depend on relationships between people, they have a context in social existence and only arise from such an origin. Andrea, for instance, the hero of *Gestern*, indulges in a life of impulsive sensuousness; the only reality is the fleeting moment, and he hates the sentimentality that seeks the stability of memories and loyalties, as if "yesterday" could be prolonged into present and future. But when his mistress is unfaithful his revulsion shows that there is a flaw in his philosophy. This is a dramatic moment, precipitated by his connection with another person. His speeches elaborate thoughts and moods, but they lead up to a crisis in which relations between two human beings disturb the feelings and impulses of one. Moods in this connection are not only lyrical, and the issue is more than simple evocation of sentiment or pathos or refinements of egoistic feeling. They are placed in a dramatic context.

Der Tor und der Tod illustrates still more strikingly how much Hofmannsthal's "Stimmungen," far from being an end of poetry, are part of a dramatic statement of life. The drama is played out between Claudio and Death; the other figures—mother, girl, friend—are phantoms. The symbolical method is obvious, for an action that goes on in Claudio's soul. It achieves a subtle and intense combination of "lyrical" mood and drama, for whilst in one sense the play is the continuous monologue of Claudio's feeling, the symbols externalize the very tense drama of his awakening to life a the moment of death.

shudder; when the warm tide of feeling rose and filled your trembling spirit, when the sudden dart of light mirrored yourself in the world's immensity, and you surrendering to the dance of things embraced the world as yours; in every hour that was great and true, thrilling through your earthly form, it was my power, sacred and mysterious, reaching your spirit in its depths.

Der Tor und der Tod is the most celebrated of the lyric dramas, and as the product of a nineteen-year-old youth it is one of the most remarkable performances in literature. Part of its force lies in its multifold suggestiveness. The commonest interpretation has been to read it as a document of the *décadence* by fastening on Claudio's central characteristic: a precious and over-refined taste for esthetic sensation, coupled with sterility in natural feelings. There can be no doubt that Claudio is an esthete, and as a victim of faulty integration is a type of "decadent" in the sense of the nineties. But Hofmannsthal's play is not on that account a pure expression of decadent sensibility as some critics aver; for that we have to look to Huysmans and Wilde, to Des Esseintes and Dorian Gray. Hofmannsthal's portrayal includes a criticism. The title dubs Claudio a Fool, and the whole meaning of the picture is in the self-awareness of Claudio that his life is vacuous. Hofmannsthal illumines the loss of integrity and completeness; and the multi-suggestiveness of this short work lies in the fact that Claudio is a symbol of that loss wherever it occurs, whether in the individual, or in the artist, or in society; and at that time it was occurring in all these three spheres. Its symptom in the artist was the sacrifice of an honest relation with life to esthetic pretence and frivolity. Its symptom in society was the acute conflict between spiritual and material values, one aspect of which was the divorce between poet and society. Hofmannsthal certainly understood estheticism; but his dramatic judgement of Claudio is a criticism of the esthete in himself and a sign that he sought integrity. And in his later work, particularly in *Jedermann* and *Das Grosse Welttheater*, he was to rediscover, in one form at least, integrity for the relationship between poetry and society.

Such a reading of *Der Tor und der Tod* is important both for Hofmannsthal and for history. Yet I think the play derives a great deal of power from something much simpler than the analysis of estheticism. It is always found astonishing because of its precocity. But if we analyse it more closely, we observe that its poetic virtuosity and its knowledge of life are precocious, but the emotional experience that makes it vital as drama is in fact that of a young man. It is youth that is most susceptible to the anguishing thought that one might die without having lived. Whatever the particular terms of Claudio's character, and whatever the "meaning" of the play, it feeds on this universal emotion and acquires through it a positive force and a poetic lustre which not only make the drama of the esthete effective but perhaps also transcend it.

The "lyric dramas" were followed by a three-act play, *Die Hochzeit der Sobeide,* which in themes and manner is still closely related to them, though the dramatic does predominate over the lyric. After that Hofmannsthal's work offers peculiar difficulties to criticism, because he developed neither as a lyric poet nor as a straightforward dramatic poet, but instead devoted his main energies to writing works which strike one at first as curiously if not bewilderingly dissimilar in subject and manner: opera-texts, some serious, some comic, some a mixture of both; the two religious plays *Jedermann* and *Das Grosse Welttheater;* and comedies of a very delicate poetic quality but rather too slender for successful stage performance, and written, moreover, in prose.

Here are indications enough of an intellectual life and an artistic sensibility that were extremely complex. The salient feature is that all these three kinds of writing, together with the lyric dramas, are founded in the theatre, and yet none of them is orthodox dramatic poetry like Shakespeare's or Grillparzer's or Racine's. They seem to constitute an exploration of possible forms for the theatre.

The clue to this phenomenon lies principally in a peculiar relationship between diverse elements of Hofmannsthal's artistic personality. There was in him first a poet of extreme esthetic impressionability, seen most clearly in the lyric dramas, seen also in a certain disguise in many of his prose essays on general and artistic subjects. The early pieces show a virtuosity in which it is difficult to separate sensuous responsiveness from technical facility, and which is to the last degree astonishing. Jumping any apprenticeship, he is from the start a master of mellifluous language, poetic phrase and apt imagery, of a readiness and fluency and movement that never falter; but these qualities are the sign, not of the true technical self-possession of the mature artist, but of the utmost vivacity of response to impressions and poetic thoughts of all kinds. It is a virtuosity of sensuousness that is without backbone, and it ends with the poet being controlled by, instead of controlling, memory and associative fancy; inundated by impressions and swept along by his own facility, he finds himself a prisoner in an autonomous verbal world, cut off from life and truth by the gift that should reveal them. It is the quality in Hofmannsthal most closely related to "estheticism."

But there was also in him a writer distinguished by intellectual coolness and lucidity, by a disposition to philosophical irony that is more at home in comedy and prose than in poetry. It is an aspect that is already apparent in the lyric dramas, in most of which there is often a curious contrast between the poetic texture and an insistent precocious knowledge of life expressed in the dramatic point of the whole. This side of Hofmannsthal presents a moralist with a didactic interest in general truths, an interest that persists throughout his work. Quite early he speaks of what seems to him to be "a favourite form": to take a character with a given set of ideas and put him in a situation that forces him to revise them. Such ironical awareness determines the conception of some of the lyric dramas and leads to the later comedies, *Cristina's Heimreise* and *Der Schwierige*. His didacticism and preoccupation with general truths appear also in the moral and metaphysical atmosphere of *Jedermann* and *Das Grosse Welttheater*. It has been insufficiently appreciated that Hofmannsthal's originality in subject-matter derives mainly from this source.

There was thirdly in Hofmannsthal a mystic who faced him with his greatest problem of form, because he led him away from words which were the immediate medium of his genius; but took him towards theatre and music where he was forced to collaborate. The mystic in him–the *Letter of Lord Chandos* is the document of this artistic crisis, and perhaps also the mysteriously symbolic *Das Bergwerk zu Falun*–felt that there was a world of spirituality higher and deeper and freer than words allow for. Language is not only insufficient to communicate this world but it is a barrier to it, a turbid medium that distorts and obfuscates. The fictive Lord Chandos takes the logical step and declares his intention of writing no more poetry; and it would be simple indeed, though less interesting, if Hofmannsthal had done the same. But the finality of this step is part of the intense expression of the letter, it gives completeness to a mood, making for what is really a poem in prose without involving Hofmannsthal himself in such an extreme practical decision.

This brief analysis of dominating tendencies helps us to understand how Hofmannsthal came to use such varied methods, as lyric drama, morality play, allegory, comedy, and opera texts, the latter again highly coloured and dramatic like *Elektra*, or delicately sentimental and comic like *Der Rosenkavalier;* and a certain unity of effort begins to appear amidst the differing inspiration. All these works are essentially poetic conceptions, they rely on the collaboration of various arts, and the medium of collaboration is theatre. There is no name for this composite and elastic form that Hofmannsthal developed for his complex inspiration, and the only way to indicate it briefly would be to call it a poetry of theatre, borrowing a phrase from Cocteau. Hofmannsthal himself sometimes uses the word "opera" in a loose extended sense. When we find him calling the second part of *Faust* an "opera," or concurring eagerly in Novalis's description of Goethe's *Märchen* (Fairy-tale) as a "narrated opera," then it is obvious that he is trying to indicate by means of this term a unique ideal of form that he had in mind.

Behind all this is Hofmannsthal's passion for the metaphysical. The attraction of allegory for him was that whilst using the language and images of life it deliberately repudiates their face-value and uses them freely as signs. *Faust Part Two* and the *Märchen* are allegorical; so are his own *Jedermann* and *Das Grosse Welttheater.* The attraction of music and dance and mime for him is that they have a more intense sensuousness than words have, a more direct appeal to feeling, but at the same time touch deeper levels of life, stirring primeval fears and reverences, expressing more mysteriously the emotions of religion and a life that is unseen and unspoken. Hofmannsthal was aware of the various contributions the different arts could make, as a matter of esthetic discrimination. He felt that words generalize best; that music gives the greatest emotional intensity; whilst a single gesture of mime or dancer can express a state of mind and dramatic relations with unequalled vividness and particularity, as when for instance Nijinsky conveyed the whole nature of the Faun in a single leap. But his sense of the collaboration of the arts in the theatre is more than esthetic discrimination. It is a profound sense of ritual, cult, liturgy, and festival, which have always, both in primitive and enlightened religions, used the various arts in combination to one end. The unity of his whole conception of a composite art depends on his consciousness of the ritualistic foundations of theatre, of the festivals of popular and religious life, of the theatre as the conscious stylization of the natural dramas of life lived between the human and the divine. The discovery of theatre is the discovery of the deepest continuities in human life, the discovery of symbols that express total human community. Such a conception is no mere artificial resuscitation of something dead and gone, no mere nostalgia. It is vital and creative because it springs from Hofmannsthal's own metaphysical passion. His work lives on this twofold force, however obvious or obscured it may be in any single piece: on the one hand the ceremony, the festive occasion, the celebration in community life, rooted in the primary needs and joys of the race; and on the other his mystic feeling for the eternal in the repetition, for the typical structure of life, for the primeval and divine that links the generations of humanity. His opera-text *Elektra*, enveloped in an atmosphere of pagan religion, working up to a culmination in Elektra's frenzied dance when her revenge is accomplished, and marred not in its conception but only in its execution by a certain hysteria, is the obvious stark illustration of where the origins of Hofmannsthal's conception of theatre are to be found. *Das Grosse Welttheater* is of course the summit of his achievement in this respect. But to illustrate the breadth and variety of the idea there is *Der Rosenkavalier*, which with all its farce is built round a central ceremony, the traditional handing over to the bride of the silver rose. This in itself gives a hint of how Hofmannsthal's conception of the theatre, through its links with the varied forms of popular festival, gave him the opportunity to find an appropriate and unified expression of the different sides of his nature.

Hofmannsthal's preoccupation with the blending of the serious and the comic shows again his central artistic problem: to reconcile in some unified form very different kinds of mental and imaginative life. Shakespeare's success in this mixed esthetic effect was a source of continual delight to him, and it was no doubt a sympathetic response of poet to poet; because the blending of the two occurs at its best under the idealizing touch of poetry. But Hofmannsthal's peculiarity emerges again in the fact that for sensuous fullness and power he is willing to rely on music rather than on dramatic poetry alone. The contrast between *Cristina's Heimreise*, or *Der Schwierige* (which are in prose, but a poet's prose), and *Der Rosenkavalier*, illustrates the point. Both the former are too tenuous to have vitality on the stage. The sentiment is too delicate, the comic idea too slender and refined. They are graceful but fragile. *Der Schwierige* is really a scenic diffusion of ideas for an essay on virtue and society; it shows a rare and distinguished moral sensitiveness reminiscent of Henry James; but its beauty, emerging gravely from ironies that are tranquil and philosophic rather than passionate and dramatic, is not very consistent with the liveliness of the theatre. *Der Rosenkavalier*, on the other hand, though its content of ideas is infinitely less important than that of *Der Schwierige*, shows how much Hofmannsthal could gain, for this tendency of his artistic creativeness, by relying on music. It is the best example of a most judicious and felicitous balancing of poetry, music, and the stage, and of a blending of serious and comic elements. Its dramatic vitality has its roots in the Vienna farce tradition; but its poetic gracefulness, which permeates the buffoonery as well as the sentimental action, gives it a unique distinction in German comedy-writing. Without the music, however, it would be a light and charming frivolity, little more; with the music, as a different *form*, that is, it takes immediately high rank as operatic comedy. The farce is idealized, and sentiment of the Marschallin-Octavian relationship, insufficient for dramatic purposes alone, is given depth and completeness by the music. This piece illustrates perfectly the difference between Hofmannsthal's artistic problem and the general conception of dramatic poetry. In the latter, language is primary, the vehicle of action and character and all the concrete situations evoked; it is allied to acting and gesture, but it prescribes them, they are not an addition but an amplification of what the words themselves contain. Hofmannsthal, by contrast, goes to different sensuous elements for contributions which are to be blended into a unity. His uniqueness lies in a poetic inspiration that gives its flavour to the whole, and a poetic technique that adjusts itself to other things: stage, mime, music, dance. The verse and the language are handled with remarkable discretion, apparent at its best, for instance, in the portrayal and situation of the Marschallin:

MARSCHALLIN. . . . Die Zeit, die ist ein sonderbares Ding.
Wenn man so hinlebt, ist sie rein gar nichts.
Aber dann auf einmal,
da spürt man nichts als sie:
sie ist um uns herum, sie ist auch in uns drinnen.
In den Gesichtern rieselt sie, im Spiegel da rieselt sie
in meinen Schläfen fliesst sie,
Und zwischen mir und dir da fliesst sie wieder.
Lautlos, wie eine Sanduhr.
Oh Quin-quin!
Manchmal hör' ich sie fliessen unaufhaltsam.
Manchmal steh' ich auf, mitten in der Nacht
und lass' die Uhren alle stehen.[3]

or:

Mir ist zu Mut,
dass ich die Schwäche von allem Zeitlich en recht spüren muss,
bis in mein Herz hinein:
wie man nichts halten soll,
wie man nichts packen kann,
wie alles zerlauft zwischen den Fingern,
alles sich auflöst, wonach wir greifen,
alles zergeht, wie Dunst und Traum.[4]

[3] Time is a strange thing. You live, and you don't think of it, and it is nothing, just nothing. Then suddenly all you feel is time: round about you, inside you. It moves in people's faces, you see it in mirrors; it flows round my temples, it flows between you and me. Silent, like sand in the glass. O Quin-quin! Sometimes I hear it irresistibly flowing. Sometimes I get up in the middle of the night and stop all the clocks.

[4] It seems to me that I must feel to the depths of my heart all the weakness of mortality: we may not keep anything, we cannot hold on to anything, all the things we grasp at slip through our fingers, dissolve, vanish, like mists and dreams.

Here is an example from *Ariadne auf Naxos:*

ARIADNE (*vor sich*). Es gibt ein Reich, wo alles rein ist:
Es hat auch einen Namen: Totenreich.
(*Hebt sich im Sprechen vom Boden.*)
Hier ist nichts rein!
Hier kam alles zu allem!
(*Sie zieht ihr Gewand eng um sich.*)
Bald aber nahet ein Bote,
Hermes heissen sie ihn.
Mit seinem Stab
Regiert er die Seelen:
Wie leichte Vögel,
Wie welke Blätter
Treibt er sie hin.

Du schöner, stiller Gott! sieh! Ariadne wartet!

Ach, von allen wilden Schmerzen
Muss das Herz gereinigt sein,
Dann wird dein Gesicht mir nicken,
Wird dein Schritt vor meiner Höhle,
Dunkel wird auf meinen Augen,
Deine Hand auf meinem Herzen sein.
In den schönen Feierkleidern,
Die mir meine Mutter gab,
Diese Glieder werden bleiben,
Schön geschmückt und ganz allein,
Stille Höhle wird mein Grab.
Aber lautlos meine Seele
Folget ihrem neuen Herrn,
Wie ein leichtes Blatt im Winde
Folgt hinunter, folgt so gern.

Du wirst mich befreien,
Mir selber mich geben,
Dies lastende Leben,
Du nimmst es von mir.
An dich werd' ich mich ganz verlieren,
Bei dir wird Ariadne sein.[5]

[5] ARIADNE (*to herself*). There is a kingdom where all things are pure: and it has a name: the kingdom of the dead. (*Rising, as she speaks.*) Here, noth-

In the freedom and lightness of these passages Hofmannsthal achieves the right density and the proper rhythmic elasticity for language that is to be supported by music; an equilibrium of melody, movement, clarity, sentiment and image that is perfectly appropriate. In Wagner's opera the words and music are a unified conception, but the text is completely dependent and has no value apart from the music. Hofmannsthal's opera text is unique because it comes so near to poetic independence and yet remains conscious that music will enhance it. It is an extraordinarily fine artistic calculation, made possible by the very craftsman's facility and delicate esthetic response that are displayed in the "lyric dramas" and against the abuse of which Hofmannsthal put himself on guard.

Hofmannsthal's religious plays *Jedermann* and *Das Grosse Welttheater* are his weightiest achievements as an independent poet, in the sense that they show the greatest degree of interfusion of his creative qualities: the poetic, the dramatic, the metaphysical, the didactic, the ritualistic. To see in them a skilful adaptation of an old morality play and an old allegorical idea, the one most famous in the English version, the other in Calderon's treatment, is a superficial reading. They have the force of original poetic creations because their subject and theme are essentially Hofmannsthal's own, expressing his spirituality, and because their form suited his particular powers. The dramatic poet, moreover, has achieved here a

ing is pure! Here was promiscuity! (*Drawing her garment closer.*) But soon a messenger will come; Hermes, they call him. With his wand he directs souls, driving them on like slender birds, like limp leaves.

O fair, tranquil god! See! Ariadne waits!

O, the heart must be emptied of its wild griefs, then your looks will beckon to me, your steps before my cave, your hand will be dark over my eyes, over my heart. These my limbs will rest in the beautiful festive robes my mother gave to me; adorned, in solitude, the quiet cave will be my grave. But silent my soul will follow her new lord, like a light leaf in the wind, follow down, joyfully.

You will set me free, give me back to myself, this burden of life you will lift from me. To you I will lose myself wholly; I, Ariadne, will be with you.

greater independence by dispensing with the collaboration of music, whilst absorbing its qualities into the symbols, the rhythmic formalization of persons and action, and the evocations of ritual. The dramatic scene is on the edge of life, from which it borrows vividness and particularity whilst pointing all the time to another world of meaning. The method is moral analysis by illustration; the object is the theatre as a vehicle of religious emotion.

The interest in generalized truths that is observable in the didacticism of the early lyric dramas reappears in its mature phase; and because it is mature it is assured and forceful. Hofmannsthal's abnormality as a young poet was of an unusual kind, because he was so knowing in a worldly sense. He was precocious in his perceptions; but his precocity is in fact the sign of his immaturity, being knowledge without experience. Expressions of general truth in poetry rely for their power and effectiveness not simply on their accuracy but on the authority with which they are put forward, and that is only conferred by a gravity of experience acquired in sufficient extent and variety and deepened by repetition. To reach this stage was for Hofmannsthal, to whom generalization was natural, to find the moment of great opportunity. The instinct that took him then to the allegorical morality play is one that confirms genius. For moral generalization, religious simplification, the barest, austerest analysis of life's typical features, are of the essence of the form. In these plays the force of appropriate generalization can be traced everywhere: in the detail of the characters and speeches as well as in the conception and construction. Of the former, a single example, the entry of the King, will suffice; and it illustrates also how a certain conventionality of language is part of the plan:

KÖNIG (*tritt von links auf und schreitet auf die Mitte der Bühne zu*).

An diesem Platz ziehts meine Schritte:
Hier bleibe ich; der Herr steh in der Mitte.

Wohin ich schau, mir alles untertan
Herrschen ist Leben—alles sonst ein Wahn.
Die Gaun und Marken, kaum zu zählen,
Empfangen Glanz und Reichtum von Befehlen.
Die Berge schaun herein, die Flüsse blitzen,
Und sehn mich in ererbten Ehren sitzen.
Sei mir das Herz im Herzen eingeweiht,
Und mit der herrlichen Gerechtigkeit,
Mit dem Verstand, der Weisheit und der Stärke,
Gesegnet meine Tag und meine Werke.
Dass ich des Lands als Leu und Adler walte,
Das Hohe hoch, das Niedre niedrig halte.[6]

It is true, of course, that Hofmannsthal's subjects, themes, and interpretations of truth are the common property of Christian Europe. But that is their strength; any great human truth makes originality superfluous. It can never be commonplace in itself, but only when it is inadequately grasped or insincerely stated. The power of "sentences," the epigrammatic pointing of common experience, which dramatists used to be very fond of and which is now out of fashion, lies in this adequacy of statement that renews the truth they contain. Hofmannsthal's handling of general truth, determined by a perfectly responsive mind, is adequate and has produced genuine poetry. In these circumstances, its conformity—with the most comprehensive religious wisdom of modern times—is its power. The test is whether Hofmannsthal as dramatic poet can rise to the height of the Christian theme. The climax of *Das Grosse Welttheater* leaves no doubt about it; the scene in which the Beggar, roused by suffering and the sense of

[6] KING (*enters from the left and goes towards the middle of the stage*). To this place my steps are drawn; here I will stand; let the King's place be in the centre. Wherever I look, there are my subjects. Power is life, the rest, illusion. Fields and cities find in obedience their wealth and splendour. The hills look on, the streams flash, and behold me seated in hereditary honours. Let my heart know the secrets of the heart; and with the glory of Right and Reason, of Wisdom and of Power, let my days, my works, be blessed. Let me like the lion and the eagle rule the land, maintaining high and low in their necessary place.

social iniquity, is impelled by his resentment to use violence against the privileged. The intercession of Wisdom, portrayed by a nun, breaks the force of his revolt:

WEISHEIT. Du aber, Leben über allem Leben,
Du wunderbar Gericht, das in den Dingen ruht,
Sieh mich nunmehr für ihn die Händ erheben:
Gnad ihm, wenn er jetzt bebend vor dich trägt,
Grässlich gefärbt mit unser aller Blut,
Den Wesensschein, den furchtbar schicksalvollen,
Drein du erhabnen Willens Spur geprägt!
Gnad ihm, ihm war von deines Spieles Rollen
Die eine überschwere auferlegt!
BETTLER (*zitternd*). Wo ist der Baum?
WEISHEIT. Was für ein Baum?
BETTLER. Den ich wie Donner schlug,
Der niederkrachend euch und mich begrub!
Doch ich–
WEISHEIT. Und du?
BETTLER. Weib? Was geschah? Wo ist das Licht?
WEISHEIT. Was für ein Licht?
BETTLER. Das aus der Krone brach,
Mit einer Menschenstimme zu mir sprach!
War dies zuvor? war dies nachher? Weib–was geschah?
Dass ich nicht auf dich schlug!–Du tratest nah–
WEISHEIT. Brach da ein Licht hervor?–und
ENGEL. War das nicht
Des Saulus Blitz und redend Himmelslicht?
BETTLER. Du hobest deine Händ und betetest für mich?
WEISHEIT. Für dich!
BETTLER. Verstehend mich und mein Gericht?
ENGEL. War das nicht Isaaks Lamm, das schimmernd sank vor dich?
BETTLER. O du mein Gott!
(*Er kniet nieder, birgt sein Gesicht in den Händen.*)
ENGEL. Nach Taten, Seele war dein Drang!
Untat war nah in finstrem Wahn,
Doch herrlich ist des Spieles Gang!
Statt Untat ist jetzt Tat getan!
BETTLER. Getan?
WEISHEIT. Getan!

BETTLER. Schlug ich?

WEISHEIT. Du schlugest nicht!

WIDERSACHER. Ein Blutandrang, ein schwindelnd Flimmerlicht und alles wiederum zunicht!

(*Er wirft wütend seine Bücher zur Seite.*

Des BETTLERS *Blick, der, wieder auf seinen Füssen, wie ein Entrückter un sich sieht, trifft den Blick der* WEISHEIT, *die wieder von ihrem Platz zwei Schritte auf ihn zugetreten ist. Sie lächelt. Er lächelt auch. Sein Gesicht hat einen verwandelten Ausdruck.*) [7]

[7] WISDOM. But Thou, Life above all life, Thou whose wondrous judgement slumbers in things themselves; see, I raise my hands in his behalf. Have mercy on him, when trembling he lays before you, lurid with the blood of all his fellows, the dread and fated life that bears the imprint of Thy sublime Will. Mercy on him, to whom was given of all the parts in Thy play the most exceeding difficult!

BEGGAR (*trembling*). Where is the tree?

WISDOM. What tree?

BEGGAR. That I struck like thunder, that crashed and buried you and me! Yet I–

WISDOM. And you?

BEGGAR. Woman? What happened? Where is the light?

WISDOM. What light?

BEGGAR. That broke from the tree-top and spoke to me with a human voice! Did that come first? Or afterwards? Woman–what happened? That I didn't strike you!–You came near–

WISDOM. A light, did a light break out?–and

ANGEL. Was it not the light that burst upon Saul and spoke with the tongues of heaven?

BEGGAR. You raised your hands and prayed for me?

WISDOM. For you!

BEGGAR. Knowing me and my trial?

ANGEL. Was it not the lamb of Isaac, that glimmered and sank before you?

BEGGAR. O Lord my God! (*He kneels, burying his face in his hands.*)

ANGEL. Soul, thy thirst was for deeds! The evil deed was near in a dark illusion; but with what splendour the play proceeds! Not the evil, but the good deed, is done!

BEGGAR. Done?

WISDOM. Done!

BEGGAR. I did strike?

WISDOM. You did not strike!

SATAN. The blood boils up, a bit of a light glimmers and makes him dizzy, and everything is spoilt once more!

(*He throws away his books in a rage.–The eyes of the* BEGGAR, *who has risen to his feet and looks about him like one in a dream, meet the eyes of* WISDOM, *who has left her place again and advanced a step or two towards him. She smiles; he smiles back. His face is transfigured.*)

In the simplest economy, this passage contains the essentials: the pathos of the human situation at its most dramatic, moral illumination and spiritual victory, the transcendent continuity of the power of the Christian God.

Jedermann and *Das Grosse Welttheater* each show a certain difference of emphasis. In the former, which is more morality than allegory, the human drama predominates, and it is built up so as to bring out with the utmost vividness the terror of Everyman's situation, meeting death suddenly, sinful and unprepared. Its main difference from the old English play is first that Death is reduced to the role of messenger, and the moral ideas expressed directly by Death in a homiletic style are presented more dramatically through the agency of characters, for example, in the conversation between Jedermann and his Mother. And secondly there is a greater psychological subtlety in conformity with the more sophisticated demands of modern drama. What is typical or schematized in the person of Jedermann is effectively balanced by traits of realism in the dramatic situation.

In *Das Grosse Welttheater*, which is more allegorical, the divine drama predominates. It is a ritualistic image of the eternal drama of creation and transfiguration, symbolical in all its details, its solemnity and ceremoniousness enhanced by formalization and dance. Its controlling symbol, moreover, the world as God's theatre, is the apotheosis of Hofmannsthal's conception of the theatre. The symbolism of theatre and the symbolism of life are inextricably merged by an act of poetry placed in the service of a metaphysical idea.

I have tried to treat the case of Hofmannsthal as a problem of form rather than as one of decadence, which is the line taken by hostile critics. What emerges from such a treatment is a consistent artistic ideal and a continuous development, which contrasts with the notion that his inspiration was dependent on the *décadence* and dried up with the "lyric dramas." Each of Hofmannsthal's forms is a different attempt to find an adequate expression for elements of his imaginative and emotional life that were diverse and difficult to reconcile; to find different forms for the demands of a complex sensibility. Only an analysis that appreciates his problem as that of finding the right form—simple and compound—for a genuine but unusual inspiration can do justice to his originality and his achievement. Hofmannsthal was creative, but he needed a complex medium. The composition of creative artists being as infinitely varied as that of men's characters, those whose assortment of talents and sensibility does not fit into standard forms have to look for other forms that enable them to say what they have to say. From such circumstances arise the deviations and combinations of the various arts that add to the richness of art as a whole. Hofmannsthal came to create not a dramatic poetry in the orthodox sense, but a poetry of theatre in a special sense. If he had to rely for realizing his conception on musicians and dancers and actors—he was fortunate in meeting a composer and a producer of genius, Strauss and Reinhardt—that does not detract from his creativeness but emphasizes its originality. We are reminded of Yeats's *Plays for Dancers* and his description of them as "a different art-form." To recall in addition Cocteau's search for a *poésie du théâtre* is to see that Hofmannsthal, like these two artists, was in fact contributing largely to a particular need of the time felt all over Europe, the renewal of the theatre's poetic vitality, and doing so not by merely superimposing an art of "production" on an indifferent text, but by starting with a total poetic conception and realizing it in a complex form.

Not the least remarkable thing about Hofmannsthal's work, however, is that in solving his private problems of form, he finds at the same time a solution of two general problems of poetry in his generation and ours; poetry in relation to the social theme in drama, and to the theatre audience in the twentieth century. *Das Grosse Welttheater* is a treatment of the social theme on a metaphysical plane; and whether you agree with the religion or not, it is poetry, and stands in strong contrast to the failure of "social problem plays" to achieve poetry. Looking back over the years between 1890 and the production of *Murder in the Cathedral* in the middle thirties, the performances of *Jedermann* and *Das Grosse Welttheater* at Salzburg and subsequently all over Europe stand out as an event of great significance for poetry and theatre. Salzburg provided an ideal setting, evocative of Catholic and baroque culture, for plays that are themselves saturated with the traditions of Christian Europe, and appealing beyond religious denominations to a vast society:

Der von Palästen und Säulenbogen umschlossene Domplatz ist italienisch, fast zeitlos. Herein blicken die Berge einer deutschen Landschaft, gekrönt von einer deutschen Burg. Die Franziskanerkirche ragt daneben auf, reines Mittelalter. Die Statuen vor dem Dom sind frühes Barock. Es war der Gedanke Max Reinhardts, auf diesem Platze, vor der Fassade des Doms, das Gerüst für das Jedermann-Spiel aufzubauen. Aber als das Spiel lebendig wurde, schien es ein Gedanke gewesen zu sein, der in diesem Platz, diesem Ganzen aus Natur und Baukunst, immer gelegen war. Die Fanfarenbläser und Spielansager hatten ihren selbstverständlichen Platz zerstreut auf dem marmornen Portikus. Wie ein Selbstverständliches wirkten die marmornen fünf Meter hohen Heiligen, zwischen denen die Schauspieler hervortraten und wieder verschwanden, wie ein Selbstverständliches die Rufe "Jedermann" von den Türmen der nhen Kirche, von der Festung herab, vom Petersfriedhof herüber; wie ein Selbstverständliches das Dröhnen der grossen Glocken zum Ende des Spiels, das Hineinschreiten der sechs Engel ins dammernde Portal, die Franziskanermönche, die von ihrem Turm herunter zusahen, die Kleriker in den hundert Fenstern des Petersstiftes, wie ein Selbverständliches das Sinnbildliche, das Tragische, das Lustige, die Musik. Selbstverständlich war das Ganze den Bauern, die hereinströmten zuerst vom Rande der Stadt, dann von den nächsten Dörfern, dann von weiter und weiter her. Sie sagten: "Es wird wieder Theater gespielt. Das ist recht." [8]

Hofmannsthal deliberately attempted to rediscover the cultic power of the theatre, and he achieved it with the festival play that has its roots deep in the religious and ethical consciousness of society, and in a spontaneous popular impulse towards the theatre. Most of the attempts at a poetic drama in this century have sprung from minority interests and have found only an exclusive audience; and we recall how Yeats in working out his ideals accepted this peculiarly modern condition. But Hofmannsthal, with *Jedermann* and *Das Grosse Welttheater*, succeeded in the broader aim. He created a dramatic symbol that united a whole society and enveloped it in a poetic situation.

[8] The Cathedral Square, framed by palaces and colonnades, is Italian, almost timeless in character. The hills of a German landscape, crowned by a German castle, look on. Near by rises the Franciscan Church, quite medieval. The statues in front of the Cathedral are early baroque. It was Max Reinhardt's idea to set up in this square, in front of the Cathedral, the stage for *Everyman*. But when the play came to life it seemed that the idea had slumbered in the place itself, this unity of nature and art. It seemed natural to find the trumpeters and heralds distributed under the marble porch; natural, too, the fifteen-feet marble saints, from between which the players made their entrance and exit, natural the cries of "Everyman" from the towers of the near-by church, the castle, the cemetery of St. Peter; natural the drone of the great bells at the end of the play, the six angels sweeping into the dim cathedral door, the Franciscan monks looking down from their tower, the priests in the hundred windows of the St. Peter chapter house; natural all the symbols, the tragedy, the comedy, the music. To the country people, too, it all seemed natural, as they streamed first from the outskirts of the town, then from the neighbouring villages, then from far and wide. They said: "There is a play to be seen again. That is as it should be."

TRAGEDY, COMEDY AND CIVILIZATION

> Vollkommenheit ist die Norm des Himmels, Vollkommenes wollen die Norm des Menschen. GOETHE.

TRAGEDY has never been associated so explicitly with the idea of civilization in the way that comedy has. The relation of the latter to the refinement of manners is traditionally accepted, and the degrees of the relation range from the simplest formula for inculcating precepts of behavior to the most delicate give-and-take between poet and audience. In more primitive forms of comedy even plain speaking, homilies and threats are not without their uses. But for high comedy, as Meredith wrote, "a society of cultivated men and women is required wherein ideas are current and the perceptions quick, that he [the comic poet] may be supplied with matter and an audience." The audience that this sentence describes—urbane, intellectual, discriminating—seems to be well on the way to a happy civilization, and comedy merely reinforces a movement towards balanced and refined living that has already begun. For this point of view it is the obvious paradox of comedy that it is both a symptom and an agent of civilization.

Meredith offers no direct comments on what happens to tragedy in such a situation, but judging by the general note of his Essay, one might infer without doing his argument violence that he thinks where comedy has installed herself men are on the way to being beyond the reach of tragedy. We have to go back to Schiller for a forthright statement of this idea, though he makes it from a different angle. He says in the essay, "Über naïve und sentimentalische Dichtung," that comedy has a higher end in view than tragedy and would make all tragedy superfluous and impossible if it succeeded in achieving it. "Its end is identical with the highest after which it is man's business to strive, to be free from passion, always to see the world and himself clearly and serenely, to attribute more to chance than to destiny, and rather to laugh at inconsequence than to rage or weep at wickedness." This is a handsome tribute to comedy from a tragic poet in whose work there is scarcely a trace of the comic view, and as it stands the logic of the argument is unexceptionable. And yet if all men achieved this "highest end" would there be anything left to laugh at, except such a consummate burning of boats? This may be the reason for the eminently discreet reservation Schiller makes—*if comedy succeeded in achieving its end.* The time in which we live cannot be said to have lessened the pertinence of this reservation. It is interesting to note how pessimistic Meredith in his turn really is about the chances of high comedy and in consequence of high civilization. He makes such demands of "subtlety and delicacy" in the comic poet, and a "corresponding acuteness" in the audience, that he is forced to observe "we count him during centuries in the singular number." For so much fervour about the benign comic spirit as is manifested in his Essay, it is a thin harvest. Yet who would disagree?

In view of Schiller's decisive reservation and Meredith's implied pessimism, it seems profitable to turn aside for the moment from this theoretic consummation of comedy. Instead we might try to do two things: reaffirm the closeness of tragedy and comedy, and define for ourselves again what tragedy has to do with civilization. Not comedy alone, but both these arts, spring from the tension between our imperfect life and our ideal aspirations. They exist together in their dependence on the contradictions of life. They are parallel expressions, in different keys, of our idea of what is good. Because they are arts, and because they have moral implications, they are a constituent of civilized consciousness as distinct from practical civilized behaviour. A reconciliation on this double basis is necessary, because on the one hand the obvious practical "uses" of comedy can obscure the fact that it rests, like any other art, on a spiritual vision which has an independent esthetic justification; and because, on the other hand, the *lack* of an obvious "use" for tragedy, its apparent esthetic self-sufficiency, can obscure the fact that it rests on a foundation as essentially and profoundly moral as that of comedy. The one is as much a matter of art, and of morals, as the other.

It is easy to forget that when we speak of tragedy and comedy we are not referring to things or events, but to judgements—particular ways of looking at things and events—depending on the moral sense. The raw material of human situations, what we call "life," is, apart from the conclusions we come to when we think about it, quite neutral. Even the presence of death, which is of great importance in drama, makes no difference in life, for it is part of its movement, it is impersonal; if we subtract human feeling and thought there is only the ever-moving limitless flux. Importance devolves upon death only from our judgements of value; downfall and destruction are significant in relation to what is good in human character and achievement. It is when the raw material of life is subjected to judgement in this way that tragedy and comedy arise, and it is obvious that there is a good deal in life that is potentially comic and tragic at one and the same time. Just which way one sees it is determined by various things; by temperament, by the alternating play of intellect or feeling, by our moods. Even a raw material with quite catastrophic possibilities can yield comic aspects by the exercise of selective judgement.

These origins of tragedy and comedy give them a particular character within poetry and art generally. Any work of art may have moral implications, but not necessarily. Poetry, the novel, the plastic arts satisfy us if they reflect life and nature with vividness and truth, clarifying our sensuous experience; this primary aim has nothing to do with morals. Tragedy and comedy, however, are in a less free position. Their subjects are not only "seen" sensuously but they are seen in a particular way in reference to good and evil. They are initiated by a moral experience. Their vision of life is shaped at the outset by a moral judgement. The idea of a "pure" esthetic experience, uncontaminated by extra-esthetic factors, is of no application where these two branches of literary art are concerned. What in other circumstances might disturb the artistic vision is here its foundation. Moral judgement is not an extraneous element but a constituent one. It is itself a formal value.

If we insist again that this view applies to tragedy quite as much as to comedy it is because in recent years, under the influence of a sharp anti-moral bias in life altogether, the tendency has been to forget how profoundly moral the atmosphere of tragedy is. Attention has been concentrated on what is called the "experience" that tragedy offers us. "Tragedy may teach us to live more wisely; but that is not why we go to it; we go to have the experience, not to use it," says Mr. Lucas in his interesting book on the subject. It is an alluring statement, appealing with ingratiating directness to some pride of esthetic detachment in us. It rises lightly above the practical problem of living; yet who has a practical problem if not Antony, Othello, Brutus? It is above all an incomplete statement. For it leaves quite out of account the equipment we take with us, and must take, when we go to the tragic spectacle. It is only our consciousness of moral values, which exists apart from tragedy, that enables us to know tragedy when we see it. If we are innocent of right and wrong, of good and evil, tragic meanings would be lost on us. The tremendous "experience" would be reduced to a succession of exciting sense-impressions. If we recognize this we shall be forced to resist heroic or dionysian views that present tragedy as a sheer glorification of "life," as an a-moral variation upon the theme "what a piece of work is man!"

The point cannot be evaded either by placing the centre of gravity in the religious understratum of tragedy. It is very difficult to conceive religion without morals. Moreover, the vaguely religious feelings of mystery, of the inscrutability of destiny and the workings of human action, of awe at what happens to Oedipus and Lear, Antigone and Hamlet, these are all germane to the experience, but they only arise because our moral aspirations are flouted. We face a mystery; but the point of the mystery is that it challenges our conceptions of good, our whole view of what ought to be in its contrast to what is. *Oedipus Tyrannus* certainly brings home to us the unfathomable force of destiny and helplessness in face of it. But why is it so terrible if not because Oedipus is involved in the most heinous wrongs, patricide and incestuous marriage with his mother? The transcendental sense of destiny is in itself a pleasant sensation; it becomes mysterious and tragic when evil and a judgement about evil are present. There is an astonishing scene in *King Lear* that reinforces what we have said about *Oedipus Tyrannus*. It is that in which Lear, scarcely rescued from the fury of nature, his ideas scattered by suffering, conducts a trial of his daughters. It is an illumination that produces from the sub-conscious the effects of order. At the moment of greatest breakdown we are given a judgement that represents amidst chaos the memory of civilization. Moral assumptions are at the centre of tragedy.

Accepting this view it becomes clear that tragedy depends on a feeling that the poet shares with his audience. He presupposes as the comic poet does a moral sensitiveness in the spectator of the same kind as he possesses himself. They both depend on the moral outlook of the whole community.

That tragic values are created by the philosophy and religion of society is another truth that has ceased to be self-evident. For since the "romantic age," perhaps since the Renaissance, it became customary to expect poets to be "original" in their thought as well as in poetry, and this led in tragedy to the idea that the poet creates a particular tragic conception of his own. The idea has been repeated so often and with such a cumulative power of suggestion that we end by holding it to be the most considerable source of inspiration and excellence. Here is to be found, on the contrary, the least part of the poet's invention. Tragic conception derives from moral dispositions that are part of the material he takes from society. The Greek poets did not create the morality and religion on which their drama rests; but they clarified them by showing life penetrated by them. Shakespeare did not add anything to the "thought" of his time; he measured life against the finest ethical sensibility he, and society, knew. Racine does not invent new moralities; he presents subjects in which the passions break the moral order established by high human traditions. Their poetry, their power of statement, is their originality; their *sense* of tragedy is something they have in common with their audience, taking its origin in the moral impulse of the whole human community. Why is there, for instance, no such thing as eccentric tragedy? There are eccentric books and poems and paintings, which attract and repel tastes with equal violence. They are creations of individuals, and even those who are repelled cannot always deny their imaginative power. But eccentric tragedy is a contradiction in terms. The poet here works not in the material of personal fantasy but of human life. The actions, passions, suffering of men in their relations with one another bind him to *their* laws and suppress *his* fancy; and the highest function of his imagination in this case is the illumination of the world outside himself. A poet trying to create his own tragic values enters the arena of opinion; his audience loses its cohesion and emotional unity; we disagree with his opinion and are insensible to his tragedy. All subjects that deal with the exceptional or the pathological case—the subjects of Kleist, for instance, and some of Strindberg—lose their tragic power; at the most they arouse the curiosity and pathos that characterize the bystander and not the participant.

In deriving tragedy from the moral aspirations of the community we discover its relation to civilization. For what it takes from the traditions of society it gives back to society assembled to see it. It focuses in the spectators the highest moral consciousness of the human community of which they are a part, so that in the reception of tragedy the community is sensitized to civilization. Under the emotional corrective of the tragic poet society agrees upon the essentials of good and evil, and is purged of its passions and injustice. At the price of vicarious suffering and death it is raised above its own life and released from the chains of everyday trial and appetite. The sense of perfection and imperfection, of nobility and degradation, of right and wrong, is retrieved, and retrieved as a social sense. The community sees good and evil inextricably confused, good defeated by evil; but it sees what good is, and carries away the knowledge chastened yet in triumph.

The moral standards of our time are so chaotic that we seem to have lost any traditional basis of tragedy. Of the three important English tragedies of the last twenty years, two—*Murder in the Cathedral* and *The Family Reunion*—are essentially Christian in conception, and in the sense that our society rests ultimately on Christian foundations, they belong to the community. But it is at least debatable whether their scope is not too narrowly Christian for them really to belong to the *whole* community of the present day. The third—*Trial of a Judge*–which certainly does refer to the community at large, is precisely the tragedy of the *loss* of moral standards. Some of this loss, or it might be denial, of moral sense is due to fear of it, following upon the breakdown of a particular system of social morality. It is the relativism with which we make shift at the moment that leads to purely "esthetic" attitudes to tragedy, with the individual in the forefront, and supported by a too simple theory of pleasure. Moral relativism produces an atomized audience and it is quite consistent that in our age the novel should be a more flourishing form than tragic drama. On the other hand, the new moralities of political parties are also an insufficient basis for tragedy, because although they provide social cohesion it is sectional and not human, particular and not general, programmatic not universal.

By insisting on its moral atmosphere and its source in the traditions of society, we reconcile tragedy with comedy and oppose the separation that the thought of Meredith and Schiller seems to imply. The two arts refer in different ways to the same thing: the illusive image of our humanity. It is our faith that we progress, however slowly, towards finer civilization. But as long as there is imperfection these forms will flourish side by side as they have always done, in Greece, in Elizabethan England, in seventeenth-century France. Even if we imagine a vast extension of civilized behaviour we might still come to the same conclusion. From isolated individual cases of refined relationships we may argue that tragedy, at least in its cruder forms, is less and less possible. But sensibilities for being the more refined are also more tender, and the mood of tragedy remains. *Three Sisters* is an example of something of this kind, and the work of Henry James, in a different medium, is full of similar effects.

The communal sense of civilization, apart from its realization, is a good in itself. We may have thought that our age was progressing rapidly; the dearth of tragic poetry we can see now retrospectively as a symptom of an interruption of progress, a failure of civilized consciousness. We are forced to rediscover this before we can do anything else. We need tragedy and comedy because they are symptoms and agents of it. There are of course other channels of civilized consciousness; the philosopher and the religious mind proceed by thought and worship. Their way involves, however, withdrawal from life; they strain towards an after-life, ecstasy in God, a humble or proud suspension of life in contemplation. The peculiar distinction of tragedy and comedy is that they are hand in hand with life, yet free from it; making the gross material itself yield the image of refinement. It is the happy paradox of their character to combine the sensuous pleasure of living with the moral pleasure of aspiration. With a miraculous virtuosity they reconcile the two halves of our nature and become the sign of civilized feeling.

GOETHE'S VERSION OF POETIC DRAMA

DRAMA, and particularly verse drama, has had a very checkered course since its great days in the sixteenth and seventeenth centuries. It would be difficult to give reasons; what makes an art flourish at a particular time and not at others is one of the thornier questions that criticism has to face. Two things can be said about drama, however, with some degree of certainty. It flourished most when printed books were not numerous, and few people learned to read. It came therefore by quite natural means to hold a high place in the entertainment world; and though this of course does not explain poetic quality, it is reasonable to think that it helped the poets to get their poetry across. And that leads us to the second point. The audience that was thus secured easily for the theatre exerted influence on the entertainment itself. Some features of Elizabethan plays, such as the accumulation of horrors and the partiality for scenes of broad comedy, even in tragic plays, can be attributed to the demands of the spectators. Later, the audience of the French classical theatre, with a leaven of learning and a more disciplined taste, influenced the choice of subject and the conventions. When these conditions are absent, good poetic drama survives only as an act of literary assertion. If competition from another sort of entertainment is strong, as was to be the case with the novel, and if the audience lacks cohesion, or purpose, or a trained taste, then the form loses its unity of entertainment and poetry, and takes two directions for two levels of taste, a popular one and a refined one, with the latter playing the losing game. Attempts to revive poetic drama have in these circumstances the character of conscious literary judgment imposing itself on the theatre; and even if great genius achieves some success, its products seem curiously detached and have an air of literary and social homelessness.

It was in such a situation that Goethe and Schiller entered the theatre. Their plays show very little give-and-take with an audience. They are composed on an ideal plan, developed solely by themselves from distant literary models—Shakespeare, the Greeks, Racine—and imposed on an institution in which very ordinary sentimental plays and chivalrous romances never for a moment ceased to flourish. Goethe's first important play, *Götz von Berlichingen*, owed more to literary and lyrical enthusiasms of the *Sturm und Drang* than to impulses from a living theatre. In his succeeding plays, the extreme degree of personal choice in the subjects is a symptom of the position. Shakespeare, by and large, did write the same sort of play as his contemporaries wrote. But where, in Goethe's case, is there amongst contemporary writing a play that by its nature is like *Egmont*, or *Iphigenie auf Tauris*, or *Torquato Tasso*, or *Die Natürliche Tochter*, or *Faust?* There is a single reasonable example, *Nathan der Weise*, a drama in verse, with a didactic aim; a play in which Lessing attempted to convey a general idea current at the time in the literary form that he thought had a greater prestige than any other. Goethe's position is not dissimilar; the link with the contemporary theatre is weak, but the relation with the field of ideas clear and direct. I said a moment ago that Goethe's subjects betray a very personal choice. But if we consider his themes rather than the plots he used we see plainly that he was working in a given atmosphere. The eighteenth century searched devotedly for a new conception of the good life, inquiring into reason and nature for its ideals, and restlessly pursuing a vision of civilization. Goethe's greatest and most characteristic plays, *Iphigenie auf Tauris*, *Torquato Tasso*, *Faust*, are variations on this theme of *Bildung*, of progress toward a culture that should embrace the individual and society.

The point is important for several reasons. It helps us to remember that Goethe's plays have a context; have a relationship to the age, and not only to him. And that leads us to the broader problem we mentioned: what determined at the time the relations between the subject and the form of drama? Was there a subject that required dramatic expression and moreover *verse* as well? The general histories of drama are shy of the plays we have just named. They don't fit in. The historian hurries past, from Lillo and Lessing, Diderot and sentimental drama, to *Götz von Berlichingen* and *Egmont*, then quickly to the *Sturm und Drang* group and Schiller, and the Ritterdrama; that is the scheme of things. How many, with the great traditions of drama in mind, have stopped to inquire why some of the finest poetry of the age appeared in two or three dramas that "don't fit in"? It is not very illuminating to tie yourself to the history of a form at the second and third level, when you ought to be asking how it stood in relation to the principal poetic inspiration. The more so, since the greatest poet was in fact using the form. That is the challenge both to history and to criticism.

Ontogenetic interpretation, powerfully reinforced by Dilthey's psychological method, has not made things easier by emphasizing Goethe's personality and underestimating the influence of literary traditions. One might be led to think sometimes that the purpose of reading him was merely to observe how rich and varied an inner life he had, and how skilfully he disembarrassed himself of his sufferings at every stage. Presented as documents of this inward process, his works cease to be more than advertisements of a spiritual heroism, or perhaps egotism. It is not to be denied that Goethe often worked closely to his own actual experiences, making a direct use of them for his poems. But it is possible to exaggerate their "personal" quality. I feel that many of Goethe's experiences, whether personal or social, were in fact stimulated by ideas of the time, because his imagination responded to them, and thus molded his actual emotions as well as his poems. It would be difficult to say with confidence whether the humanitarian feeling of *Iphigenie auf Tauris* flowed from his love for Charlotte von Stein, or whether the character of that love was not itself determined partly by the humanitarianism of the century.

We are here at grips with a subtle interplay of forces, in which Goethe's sense of values responds to certain ideas and ideals of the time, and he dramatizes that response. He uses characters and a plot, because you can't write a play without them; but they themselves do not contain the real drama. They point to an impersonal mental drama that is really the thing Goethe wants to express. The germ of the conception is to be found as early as *Götz von Berlichingen,* which is superficially an imitation of Shakespeare, but in essence an enthusiastic portrayal of a champion of freedom and "natural" justice. *Egmont* appears to be a study in character; yet Egmont, however brilliantly portrayed as a person, is still more an idea. The mainspring of his nature is a splendor of vitality and spontaneous genius that at its best is heroic, and for Goethe and his time constituted a precious value. But Egmont's assurance can also degenerate into insouciance; he lacks prudence, reason, and the disciplined statesmanship that enable William of Orange to meet the crafty calculation of the Spanish tyrants. William wins, Egmont is a victim. Yet Goethe is not satisfied with placing Egmont in a situation which because it ends tragically seems to put him in the wrong and give the palm to the wisdom of Orange. Through the peculiar and much-discussed allegorical vision at the close of the work, he justifies Egmont and restores the balance between the two men and their differing genius. Except for this close, the appearances of the play are orthodox; it seems a straightforward historical drama. But the exception is significant as the most obvious symptom of an inherent tendency in the play which was of the greatest importance for what was happening in Goethe's handling of dramatic form. We see in fact the true Goethe emerging, using a historical subject to portray something that he feels about ideals of life. It is not simply a question of how human character produces tragedy or comedy, or how life drives us into a trap, or of evil opposed to good. The play tests ideals of conduct and expresses a sense of conflicting kinds of virtue, of how different kinds of good seem to be mutually exclusive.

What is embryonic here comes to a first stage of fruition in *Iphigenie auf Tauris* and is completed in *Torquato Tasso*. In the former, Goethe's new drama of ethical sensibility receives a clear form, though in this case we do see good and evil opposed. Its basis is the existence of a sphere of innocence and purity, and on the opposing side one of passion, deceit, barbarity, and brutal action. Iphigenie is the guiltless member of a guilty race, saved by Diana from being sacrificed at Aulis, and now serving as her priestess in Taurica. She is protected and even loved by King Thoas. She lives within the sanctuary, severed from the grossness of life, kept undefiled by her office, and though she makes no claim to be more than a simple human being, she acts by a virtue that removes her from baseness and vice, and shrouds her person in sanctity and nobility. On the other side there is her family and ancestry: Tantalus and his race, with a history of presumption and crime, of tyranny and selfishness, a horrible succession of patricide, fratricide, infanticide, reaching down to the latest excesses, the adultery of Clytemnestra, the murder of Agamemnon, Orestes' revenge on his mother, the persecution of Orestes by the Furies. The tension between these two spheres gives the moral atmosphere of the piece.

It crystallizes, as you know, in a conflict in the main character, when Orestes, seeking liberation from the Furies, arrives in Taurica, and falls under the law that requires strangers to be sacrificed to the gods. Iphigenie must either recognize the gods and the barbarous ritual they demand; or defy them, and save her brother by an impious act and a cruel deception of Thoas her protector. At this point Goethe detaches his Iphigenie from the mythical material and Greek religious conceptions and makes her evolve an ethical ideal consonant with the rational and humane aspirations of the eighteenth century. She reveals the position to Thoas and stakes everything on his humanity. In a closing scene made splendid by its optimistic assertion of faith, Thoas responds to her feeling and allows the sister and brother to go back to Greece.

In this setting Iphigenie and Orestes are symbols. I mean by that something more than a reference to a so-called "experience" of Goethe's. Traditional interpretations of the work have made great play with the idea that Orestes is purified by the spiritual force of Iphigenie, and it is customary to see in this a poetic expression of Goethe's own ethical development, partly under the influence of Frau von Stein. Even Gundolf, while holding off the meaner sort of biographical commentary, and keying up the matter to a pitch of heroic magnificence, adheres substantially to this conception. It is a pity such readings are pressed so far, because they create confusion about the aims and value of poetry, and of Goethe's poetry. I have just now indicated how a chain of wickedness and guilt of indescribable horror lies behind Orestes' own murder of his mother, and all of it essential to the idea of the play. I do not know what Goethe had personally to put at the side of this. The natural excesses of exuberant youthful emotion, and a sequence of love affairs, do not seem to me to be a sufficient parallel. He may have got hints from his own lapses; but until evil in some violent form breaks out in our lives, that is all most of us have to go on to help us to understand great wickedness. Orestes is not Goethe; he is imagined. When, in the remarkable third act, we see him overcome by suffering and remorse, the scene evokes profound compassion not because of Goethe's guilt, and not only because of Orestes', but because of the guilt and evil of the whole world, here deliberately gathered together by the poetic imagination into a single symbol of trenchant force.

Similarly Iphigenie is not merely a girl who doesn't tell lies. If we take truth and deceit in this play in a literal sense, the effect is flat, and certainly so ordinary an ethical notion contrasts oddly with the munificence of ethical response which makes the triumph of the work. Truthfulness here is conceived in the absolute sense of spiritual integrity, of which adherence to truth is but the most obvious and most easily perceived aspect. It is the consistency with oneself and one's faith which gives us our defense against chaos and protects human relations against the caprice and malevolence that disrupt them. It is this that Iphigenie is concerned about when she utters her challenge to the gods: "Rettet mich, und rettet euer Bild in meiner Seele." The conventional notion of telling the truth is inadequate to describe her situation. She has to save her soul by constancy and innocence, and the choice facing her, quite beyond anything that is covered by the word convention, is that which confronts everyone who wishes to be civilized.

Following such a line of thought we escape from a certain pettiness that clings to personal interpretations and begin to apprehend a greater imaginative dimension in the play. It is impossible to think in terms of Goethe or particular characters but only of voices which echo opposing worlds and forces. Iphigenie and Orestes, in a remarkable poetic process, are each absorbed as individuals into the one ruling idea of the play, until they lose particularity as persons and exist with an intensity which is that of poetic symbol alone, all their personal being transcending itself in the impersonal spirituality of the theme. If it seems that Orestes is "purified" by his sister, that simply means here that the world in which he moves is engulfed by the light of Iphigenie's world and its potency destroyed.

Torquato Tasso amplifies and intensifies this process of poetic composition. Again we have to run counter to accepted ways of looking at Goethe's work. In the first place, the vividness of the portrayal of Tasso is to some extent misleading; though the fact that a quite pitiless censure is mingled with the pathos is enough to make one suspect that more is involved than the person of Tasso. It would be a very unsatisfactory drama if it were merely a near-tragedy about a sensitive and morbid genius. To read it in literal terms would call for a standard of judgment from the traditional dramatic form of the sixteenth and seventeenth centuries, and by that standard it is extremely faulty.[1] Secondly, it would not be quite so great a work as it is, were it simply about a Goethe conflict, objectified partly in Tasso and partly in Antonio. If, on the other hand, we go behind the persons of its surface, we see unfolding a drama remarkable for the range of its implications concerning the conflicts of our mental life and social situation. The plot, flimsy and totally inadequate as orthodox drama, is the merest pretext to suggest these conflicts. The imagination responds to the idea of freedom and creativeness, of spontaneous joys and natural happiness; social and political living, on the other hand, make imperative the different but equally justified values of disciplined manners, of propriety, of discreet wise conduct. Any ideal of the social whole requires all these values; but any reality shows them continually in conflict. This is the theme of *Torquato Tasso;* and the idea of the two souls in Goethe's breast is not the end of the piece, but the beginning. Goethe felt the division in himself, but its importance for the play is that it gave him the knowledge of the larger conflict that goes on in human society. Either side without the other falls short of completeness, whether you

[1] I think it could be argued that Goethe's interest in the psychology of a certain type of genius tended to run away with him, and I would maintain that it led to a fault of execution without altering the fundamental conception that I am here trying to expound and believe to be the most important aspect of the work.

look at it from the individual or the social point of view. Goethe shows a poet at cross-purposes not only with a man of action, but with a world of the utmost refinement. Tasso is opposed to no Machiavelli, but to Alfons and the Princess, to the human civilization that permeates their court and their lives, of which Antonio is but one part. All this cultivated Ferrara atmosphere is wonderfully portrayed; it is the essence of the play's spirit; it gives us the very image in the poise of language, manners, and conduct, of what is meant by being civilized. It is the real pivot of the drama, the point to which we refer both Tasso and Antonio, the ideal picture of a way of living that is compounded of taste and reason, of what Tasso has to give, combined with what Antonio has to give. That is why Goethe's Ferrara demands the friendship of the two men, as a symbol that disparate elements of civilization have been brought into harmonious relationship. This reconciliation is one to which we aspire, because it would in fact be integrated life. Goethe's work expresses this simple human aspiration that two sets of values should be harmonized; and at the same time a shadow falls over the scene from the sense that they might be irreconcilable, or at least that to be civilized costs you something personal, the too private world and too private joy. Hence the peculiar blend in the tones of the piece; of delicate idealizing fancy, of something that passionately suggests idyllic aims, and on the other hand a tragic sense of opportunities missed, of human imperfections not to be overcome, of prices to be paid in suffering and renunciation.

The phenomenon we observed in Iphigenie repeats itself. As the play proceeds we become more and more aware that a wholly mental world is being evolved and abstracted from a world of persons. These persons have often been criticized as unreal, and so they are if we judge by the standards of ordinary life which are here irrelevant. It is not the Princess and Alfons and Leonore that matter, finally, but the culture they incorporate; not Tasso, but the idea of imagination, liberty, spontaneity, and individual happiness; not Antonio, but the idea of discretion, political wisdom, statesmanship, right conduct. Consider what happens when we hear a passage like this:

PRINZESSIN. Auf diesem Wege werden wir wohl nie
Gesellschaft finden, Tasso! Dieser Pfad
Verleitet uns, durch einsames Gebüsch,
Durch stille Täler fortzuwandern; mehr
Und mehr verwöhnt sich das Gemüt und strebt,
Die goldne Zeit, die ihm von aussen mangelt,
In seinem Innern wieder herzustellen,
So wenig der Versuch gelingen will.
TASSO. O welches Wort spricht meine Fürstin aus!
Die goldne Zeit, wohin ist sie geflohn,
Nach der sich jedes Herz vergebens sehnt?
Da auf der freien Erde Menschen sich
Wie frohe Herden im Genuss verbreiteten;
Da ein uralter Baum auf bunter Wiese
Dem Hirten und der Hirtin Schatten gab,
Ein jüngeres Gebüsch die zarten Zweige
Um sehnsuchtsvolle Liebe traulich schlang;
Wo klar und still auf immer reinem Sande
Der weiche Fluss die Nymphe sanft umfing;
Wo in dem Grase die gescheuchte Schlange
Unschädlich sich verlor, der kühne Faun,
Vom tapfern Jüngling bald bestraft, entfloh;
Wo jeder Vogel in der freien Luft
Und jedes Tier, durch Berg und Täler schweifend,
Zum Menschen sprach: Erlaubt ist, was gefällt.
PRINZESSIN. Mein Freund, die goldne Zeit ist wohl vorbei,
Allein die Guten bringen sie zurück.
Und soll ich dir gestehen, wie ich denke:
Die goldne Zeit, womit der Dichter uns
Zu schmeicheln pflegt, die schöne Zeit, sie war,
So scheint es mir, so wenig, als sie ist;
Und war sie je, so war sie nur gewiss,
Wie sie uns immer wieder werden kann.
Noch treffen sich verwandte Herzen an

Und teilen den Genuss der schönen Welt;
Nur in dem Wahlspruch ändert sich, mein Freund,
Ein einzig Wort: Erlaubt ist, was sich ziemt.

TASSO. O wenn aus guten, edlen Menschen nur
Ein allgemein Gericht bestellt entschiede,
Was sich denn ziemt! anstatt dass jeder glaubt,
Es sei auch schicklich, was ihm nützlich ist.
Wir sehn ja, dem Gewaltigen, dem Klugen
Steht alles wohl, und er erlaubt sich alles.

PRINZESSIN. Willst du genau erfahren, was sich ziemt,
So frage nur bei edlen Frauen an.
Denn ihnen ist am meisten dran gelegen,
Dass alles wohl sich zieme, was geschieht.
Die Schicklichkeit umgibt mit einer Mauer
Das zarte, leicht verletzliche Geschlecht.
Wo Sittlichkeit regiert, regieren sie,
Und wo die Frechheit herrscht, da sind sie nichts.
Und wirst du die Geschlechter beide fragen:
Nach Freiheit strebt der Mann, das Weib nach Sitte.[2]

[2] PRINCESS. Tasso, that way we shall never, never find society. Such paths lead us astray; we wander on through solitary groves and quiet valleys, whilst our heart, bemused and spoilt, strives to create again within itself the golden age it cannot find outside, however little the attempt succeeds.

TASSO. O Princess, what a great word comes from your lips! The golden age for which each human heart yearns in vain, whither is it fled? When men like joyous flocks wandered in enjoyment over the earth; when an ancient tree in some bright meadow gave shade to shepherd and shepherdess, whilst the light branches of a sapling growth closed tenderly around love and desire; where soft streams, their sandy beds forever clear and tranquil, took nymphs in a gentle embrace; when snakes, taking fright but hurting no one, disappeared in the grass, and bold fauns fled, punished by some youthful hero; when every bird, free as the air, and every beast wandering over hill and vale, said to men: whatever pleases may be done.

PRINCESS. My friend, the golden age, we know, is past; yet good men can bring it back. And if I may confess my own view of it all: the golden age, the beautiful time, of which poets speak to us so flatteringly, existed then no more than now, it seems to me; and if it ever did, then it was surely such as we can rediscover any time. Hearts in tune still find each other and share their pleasure in the beauteous world; one word only in the motto need be changed, my friend; whatever is seemly, may be done.

TASSO. Oh! if only a general court chosen from good and noble men would declare what is seemly, instead of each believing that what serves him

When I hear this I begin to lose touch with Tasso and the Princess as persons, however vivid they are, and to feel that there is something still more important than they. I see Goethe's mind responding first to one value, and then to another, and sensible of a dilemma. But then behind Goethe's mind I become aware of the general human consciousness involved in a conflict within itself, and Goethe's mind is simply the medium that clarifies it. So it is constantly throughout this play, and it is not difficult to see that we are very close to the technique of *Faust*. First we observe persons in an exchange of sentiments, then the play of ideas and evaluations of experience gets the upper hand, and we forget the persons, to find ourselves spectators of the human mind staging an intimate drama of its own dilemmas. Conversations that seem at first to be perfect pieces of meditation, epigrams that succeed each other so naturally and yet with such startling abundance, passages that might seem to be an inappropriate irruption of didacticism into a drama of personalities, appear before long as the result of an underlying motive with a well-defined effect: they create the mental perspectives, outside time and space and particular individuals, where the real conflict, the permanent crisis, is staged. The dramatic propriety that normally rests in the relation of character and action is less important here than the sense of contrasting ideals; it is a drama that goes on behind the drama of persons. Everywhere the poetic voice transcends the limits of a scene in a plot, creating a new dramatic order. And the superb vocal style, the wonderfully sensitive thought and rhythms of the verse,

best is also right and proper. It's plain enough, a strong and clever man takes every liberty and gets away with it.

PRINCESS. If you would learn precisely what is seemly, inquire simply of noble women. For they most of all are concerned that everything that happens should be good and seemly. Propriety like a wall surrounds the frail and gentle sex. Where morality prevails, there too, do they, and where impudence takes charge they count for nothing. And if you ask of both the sexes: man aspires to freedom, woman to virtue and decorum.

which it would be easy to admire as a supernumerary effort, are seen to spring from the heart of the subject.

The essential nature of a Goethe play is a drama of symbols illustrating a drama of the search for values; and the method of *Iphigenie* and *Tasso* is the same as that of *Faust*. Nothing has been more unfortunate than the application of Shakespeare's standards to Goethe's work, suggested, as ill luck would have it, by Goethe's own early enthusiasm for him, and by the general imitation of Shakespeare on the incentive of Lessing. Shakespeare's dramatic image of life adheres to the time-and-space reality of human relations, and his foundation is a coherent personal destiny. It is, of course, true that his plays are also "symbolic," and that over and above the story we become aware of a philosophic or lyrical meditation; for no great works of poetry are without an idea, they are never simply "human stories." But even so the lyrical meditation and the objective drama in Shakespeare are correlated at all points, the meditation growing out of the very fullness and vividness of the picture of life. Goethe's picture of life in this sense is fragmentary. It is characteristic that his interest in the action-and-character kind of plot is subordinate, and compared with the greatest dramatists he is uninventive and relatively unskilled in handling dramatic material of that kind. In reading any of his plays we constantly have to overcome irritations. But the important thing is that Goethe starts from possible ideals of behavior and finds the dramatic conflict between them; and so his image of the mental drama of values is complete. He has broken with the conception of drama that was the legacy of the sixteenth and seventeenth centuries, and we should be careful not to make the mistake of criticizing his plays by the standards of Shakespeare and Racine alone. It is a new kind of drama, and in deciding whether it is a good one, we have to bear in mind that there is room for variety in the theatre. The puzzling thing about Goethe's plays is that they are neither dramas of personal destiny nor plays of ideas; yet they contain persons who are very living, and they deal with ideas all the time. Iphigenie, Tasso, Faust, are intensely vital conceptions, but the actual "plot" they are involved in is faulty and incomplete. And on the other hand the "ideas" in these plays do not mean debate, ideology, and argument, of which the persons are mere mouthpieces. The clue to the riddle lies in the kind of thought that Goethe is preoccupied with. It is thought about how to live, about what is valuable in living, about the quality of experience. Such thought is inseparably interwoven with life and decisions about life; with our emotions and our senses, with our character as well as with our intellect, and it can only be apprehended with complete clarity in visual images of how people behave. This is the secret of Goethe's poetic subtlety; for he has created these visual images. Hence it is that though he doesn't start from character in making his plays, his persons nevertheless have an intense life. They are unindividual; they are governed by generalized conceptions; they always throw light in some way on a pattern of behavior, on an ideal, or a typical aspect of experience; but they are vivid because it is living that is involved. The conflict in Goethe's drama appears projected in different persons because that is the only way to secure the dramatic picture; but behind that it lies, as I have suggested, in the mind of everyone who is at all sensitive to these things. It lay in the mind of Goethe, and all the passion and emotion with which he himself experienced moral conflict he has poured into his characters. The elements of his own actual experiences that we see reflected in his persons, and on which he certainly drew liberally and to great advantage, are parts of his dramatic method, the tools he uses to fill his symbolic persons with life, and to communicate the whole mental experience as one that takes place in the conditions of life. His essential subject is the sensitiveness of the mind to ideals, the drama of how sensibility comes to grips with values, and it is presented by a method of remarkable originality.

From this point of vantage it is easier to meet criticism of Goethe's drama, because it is clear that with his delicate inward creation Goethe also creates his own canon and makes obsolete the standards previously applicable. Iphigenie has of course been called before now, rather apologetically, a *Seelendrama*. But I think that was meant to convey the notion of a play of psychological conflict in one person, whereas Goethe's plays generalize explicitly beyond the single individual. When we have perceived his originality, the faults that orthodoxy stigmatizes matter less. All the trouble about the Iphigeneia subject from the Greek is a striking example. For the modern writer that material is very intractable. Even Racine had great difficulty in handling a subject that involved human sacrifice and the miraculous intervention of a goddess. His problem was to make a tragedy that would fit Aristotle's rule and be acceptable to reason; but in shifting the tragic emphasis from Iphigenie to another character he loses unity and his piece breaks down, leaving us with the feeling that this great master of technique is not at his best. Goethe, using the later history of the Iphigeneia, has also to face the problem of the religious framework with its gods and their commands and rites, which are so unacceptable to modern thought. He deals very cavalierly with them, and his arrangements are makeshift. But it doesn't matter finally, because the whole point is that his Iphigenie should incorporate an ethical attitude superior to barbarous cults. In the total result, therefore, we feel that he has achieved more than Racine, because he has achieved his purpose, a unity of idea. Though we have to overcome a sense of irritation, we do so in the end, not only because we see that it is important that we should do so, but because Goethe is in fact succeeding.

When we view the succession of Goethe's dramas we see the evolution of a consistent method. *Torquato Tasso* seems to me to be the pivot of the development. Under the surface orthodoxy of *Götz von Berlichingen* and *Egmont* we have observed anticipations of the method. In both those plays there is something Goethean that doesn't square with the framework Goethe took over, and looking back at them from *Torquato Tasso*, we see how they contain an embryo of his true subject. The incipient iambic verse in the close of *Egmont*, and the recasting of *Iphigenie*, take on a particular significance from this new point of view; for the convention of verse supported his imagination in its direction toward an original subject and a subtle form. The technique appears increasingly in the revisions of *Faust*, that is to say, after the writing of *Tasso*. It becomes, indeed, plain for all to see, the symbolism and allegory growing more and more obvious and elaborate. We are all perhaps in danger of reading *Tasso* literally, but no one can make that mistake with *Faust*. This work, of course, has a long history, and its various stages show the evolution of Goethe's dramatic method, and almost every degree of success and failure. The fragmentary *Urfaust* is the nearest Goethe came to a straightforward human tragedy of passion, and it is unique in his plays. The conception of the extended *Faust* is from the start a drama dealing with the awareness of values; it actually begins with Faust abandoning the intellectual sciences as one-sided and inadequate, and dreaming of an experience that would telescope the sum of life into an instant and make him see all value in a single moment. Faust himself is not a person; he is personality used by poetry to image a mental arena. Mephistopheles, Helena, Gretchen, are all saturated with symbolism. But they are living poetic figures because what they symbolize has always a reference to a way of life. They are without the particular individuality that we associate with character in real life; to that extent they are abstractions, stylizations. But what they represent are always forms of living and experiencing, to be perceived not in ideas that they might talk about but in what they are and how that is expressed in human behavior. They are therefore parallel figures to those of *Iphigenie auf Tauris* and *Torquato Tasso*. They are, of course, much more complex in their symbolism than the earlier creations; but in that we observe not a difference, but the elaboration of the same poetic method. *Faust*, moreover, insists as little on a conventional "plot" as the earlier plays, and for the same reasons: a conflict of passion, or will, or character, or fate, gives way to the conflict of values that is present everywhere in the nature and structure of human life, and in our consciousness of it.

A point is reached, of course, at which Goethe overshoots the mark and allows allegory to develop at the expense of that sense of life to which we have referred, and his work then becomes progressively more abstract and literary, and less vital as dramatic poetry. The decline is noticeable in *Die Natürliche Tochter* which satisfies neither as a human drama nor as a mental one. The method is the same, and it is outwardly emphasized by abandoning individual names and using the stereotyped "König," "Baron," and so on. But it has become abstract and schematic, just as the style, wonderful as a technical effort, has sacrificed its true foundation and become virtuosity. As time went on Goethe lost the intense personal feeling and the vivid sympathetic imagination that give the persons of the great plays, however ideally conceived, their life. His later essays in dramatic poetry, *Pandora*, most of *Faust* II, have some fine qualities; but they show the fundamental method developed without sufficient dramatic substance to justify the link with the theatre. They are often beautiful in their formal outline and provide many examples of Goethe's power of fusing philosophical and lyric statement. They tend, however, to be diagrammatic illustrations of didactic ideas, the dialogue contains more reflection than action, and the verse is too diffuse. Hofmannsthal was attracted by the "operatic" qualities of these later parts of Goethe's work; and such a suggestive analogy would imply a different relationship with the theatre which would raise interesting speculations. From the point of view of poetic drama, however, they are remote from the theatre. In his best period Goethe's generalizations were in immediate contact with experience; in the decline they easily become detached and wear too often the look of knowledge supported only by faint memories of life.

We set out with the question in our minds, what place does Goethe's drama occupy in the history of the form, and what relationship does it establish between poetry and drama in his time? We mentioned one or two factors of significance: the lack of a proper theatrical setting, or a live theatre with an audience sensitive to poetry and itself helping to shape drama, like the Elizabethans, or the French aristocracy of the *Grand Siècle*. Then we noticed the presence of a decided background of ideas, mainly ethical and educative in tendency, and far more important, when Goethe started to write, than any form of imaginative literature.

The arresting feature of this situation is that the most refined poetic sensibility of that time seized on what was most vital in its intellectual consciousness and made that the new subject of drama, or, to put it another way, extracted from it its *dramatic* aspect. Herder and Schiller could teach and preach; say what was true, what was beautiful, as a matter of intellectual judgment. Goethe absorbed their climate of ideas; you can't read his plays without recollecting Lessing, Herder, Voltaire, Rousseau, and Winckelmann, all devoted to the search for civilized living. But his distinguishing mark is that he never thinks without feeling; the apprehension of ideas is connected at every point with sensibility; thought and ethics are always impregnated with imagination and transformed into the kind of experience that calls for poetry as its natural expression. He effected a subtle alliance between ethical ideas and the contexts in life through which they are perceived and felt; and drawing on this he was able to portray in drama the general consciousness in the act of being invaded by ideas and ideals; the sense of values evolving; the mind in the very process of being sensitized to truth, poetry, civilization, and subjected to all the difficulties and conflicts the process brings with it. His plays are full of the dramatic tensions of our minds trying to shape our lives.

This distinguishes him from Schiller, for whom it can be claimed that he put across ideas, but not that he created poetic images like Tasso and Faust. Goethe has suffered from the fact that Schiller has always been a popular success in the theatre, and I feel that my argument lays upon me an obligation to make at least a short comment on their comparative merits as dramatists. I do not want to disparage Schiller; we know well enough why he should be respected. But in judging his work there are at least as many qualifications to be made as in the case of Goethe. The fact is, of course, that there is no German dramatist without spikes; none whom we can admire with abandon as we admire Shakespeare and Racine for their wonderful fusion of acting, drama, and poetry. But no dramatist anywhere in Europe after Racine has reached their level. The most we get is an interesting development of single features. Grillparzer and Ibsen succeeded more than anyone else in preserving a tense action while exploiting something new in the form. Goethe added a new poetic intensity at the expense of the plot of incident. Schiller maintained a strictly theatrical effectiveness within a framework derived from Shakespeare. In the broad sense that he associated drama with the ideas of the time, he worked on similar lines to Goethe. But his method was to pick out a few of the grand ideas that interested him and elaborate them in a rhetoric both of language and of theatre, frankly enthusiastic and tendentious, and penetrating successfully to a wide public. Goethe found the poetic form not for this or that idea, but for the whole ethical response of the time; not for slogans and precepts but for the actual spiritual process. From Schiller's plays we deduce ethical sensibility; in Goethe's we see it imaged. When it comes to a stirring action in the theatre, Schiller has it, obviously. But on the formal side he is without interest; his plays are orthodox, that is to say, imitative, both as program pieces, and as tragedies. *Wallenstein* is always judged to be his best play because it is the least tendentious, and comes nearest in fact to what a generalized notion of Shakespearian history and tragedy lead you to expect. Technically speaking, Schiller looked backwards, and therefore his popular success in the theatre can scarcely be urged against Goethe's originality. Schiller's drama is defective by the standards it tries to conform to, and for our finer judgment it is saved principally by our sense of a noble personality behind it. Goethe's plays, on the other hand, deliberately abandon orthodox standards because they have a new poetic purpose.

If his conception made it inevitable that he should deviate from well-established notions about stage drama, it restored vitality to a great form, added something new, and preserved the unity of poetry and drama. The *Rührstück* and the *Ritterdrama* were popular entertainments; at the most the former was associated with the moral explorations of the age at a debased level. The *Sturm und Drang*, dramatizing with a great deal of fuss, was no more than a minor German eddy in the spiritual life of a European age. Goethe's verse plays, pushed aside as curiosities by historians of drama, are in fact central, because they show poetic and dramatic genius applied to the main stream of thought, and incidentally give to German poetry a European status. Their heterodoxy is the consequence of a vital subject matter, the adaptation that a traditional form, handled by genius, always makes to meet the demands of a new outlook.

We do not wish to claim too much for Goethe's drama; but not too little either, and in the past it has been appreciated abundantly as the work of Goethe, not enough as a contribution to poetic drama. The new subject was not so easy to treat for the theatre as the old drama of will, passion, and fate. It is inward, admittedly less productive of external incident and theatrical effects, it is delicate and sensitive. But it is tense and exciting, and extends the possibilities of the form. These plays are often said to be for reading and not for acting. Yet their language urges as irresistibly to speech as that of Shakespeare and Racine. We observe, moreover, that Goethe anticipates one of the great developments of modern thought and poetry. We no longer think of art in simple naïve ways, having become much more self-conscious about our psychological processes. We think, and we observe how we are thinking; see, and observe how we are seeing. We look for forms of experience as well as for contents, for images of mental movement as well as of external nature. The simple drama of character and plot no longer compels innocent attention, as modern dramatists know. Something of this complexity is present in Goethe. His drama shows an early stage in the development of self-consciousness, and his genius is apparent both in the anticipation and in the bold exploration of a new form for it. Surveying the course of dramatic poetry in Europe, we see that he transformed drama in order to attune it to a new major phase of experience. At its best, the form he found, based, like all great drama, on the poet's voice, is one of the subtlest the dramatic imagination has yet evolved.

A NOTE ON GEORG BÜCHNERS' PLAYS

READING Büchner's plays without special previous study one is struck quite especially by three features, the language, the tendency for feeling to be focused in flitting scenes of great poignancy, and a general mood of disillusion and futility, relieved here and there by moments of human tenderness. The language is a strong and supple dialogue prose, very alive, very near to spoken everyday idiom, often brutally direct, hard and spare, but often yielding to gentler sentiment and touched with vivid poetic images. The scenes that impress one so much are nearly always quite brief, intensively evocative of terror, despair, or anguish, and in consequence moving and beautiful. The general mood of pessimism includes feelings ranging from a coarse cynicism to a more dignified tragic despair. This mood can be rather futilely depressing, but it is sincere; it shows a genuine revulsion of feeling.

Having received these fresh impressions one is impelled, in the interests of a better understanding of *Dantons Tod* in particular, to look into Büchner's politics. At once the sky darkens. Too much happened, and too quickly, with Büchner's political activities; and then he died. No one can really know whether he had *Weltschmerz* because of his political views, or his particular politics because of his *Weltschmerz*. One turns, for instruction, to the literature of the subject, and though one finds much helpful information and illuminating comment, one remains aware of an oppressive, unresolved problem, seen most clearly in the way critical views, falling roughly into two groups, the metaphysical and the sociological, are too deliberately opposed to each other, too exclusive, too intent on a unitary system of thought in one direction or the other. Yet most critics, except the more cautious Knight and Sengle, manage to admire Büchner almost as though he were a sacred person.[1]

Turning back to the plays one finds in them, especially in *Dantons Tod*, a good deal that is fundamentally unclarified, if one tries to make it fit into a neat, logical pattern in relation to his political activities and his declared opinions. But one is then, in my view, more than ever convinced of what makes his literary strength in the slender and fragmentary, but extremely moving, intermezzo that he contributed to German dramatic literature, and to which in fact both kinds of listeners, the sociologists and the metaphysically minded, may respond.

I think it helps with *Dantons Tod* if one faces up to the possibility of its being not a unified but a very un-unified work. We have Sengle's[2] authority for saying that it is not a "historical drama" in the traditional sense; that Büchner is using history to prove his own desperate view of men as the victims of the *Fatalismus* of history. Nevertheless it seems to me that there *is* a historical play in *Dantons Tod*, and one in which a true phase of the French Revolution can be made to yield a symbolic meaning about the revolutionary process in general. In this part of the play there is a sketch for a grandiose tragedy of human effort. In the opposition between Danton's party and Robespierre's we see focused the moment in the Revolution where judgment is divided as to ends and means, success and failure. The advantages of the new order are not immediately gained, the promises not

[1] Full bibliographical information is given in Horst Oppel's excellent *Forschungsbericht. Stand und Aufgaben der Büchner-Forschung. Euphorion*, XLIX (1955).

[2] Friedrich Sengle, *Das deutsche Geschichtsdrama* (Stuttgart, 1952), pp. 132ff.

fulfilled. In the name of the same initial idealism some wish to call a halt, whilst others wish to go forward with still greater vigor. The picture is familiar enough to us now: the means of bloodshed and terror begin to negate the ends of social justice, and the original idealism of revolution is dissipated either in the rigid, Puritanical fanaticism of a Robespierre or a Saint-Just, or in the sense of futility, of human helplessness amidst forces unloosed and events set racing, focused in a Danton. It is the stage in revolution when the conflict of revolutionaries versus social enemy is transformed into that of revolutionary versus revolutionary. This aspect of the work, impressively stark in its insight and originality in the literature of Büchner's day, is one about which we can agree with sociological critics like Lukács without committing ourselves to doctrinaire views. It gives the play an appeal that becomes particularly effective at other periods of history where similar processes are at work. The Spender-Rees translation of *Dantons Tod* in 1939 shows how this happened in England in the thirties, the decade of ideological conflict, in which particularly the humane and liberal outlook was felt to be more and more helpless against the inherent power of massive social movements. There are instants, including the end of Act II and Act III, when *Dantons Tod* touches a grandeur that derives from the momentary vision of historical process and of the tragic in all revolutions.

But this is not Büchner's whole play; he would indeed have done better to devote himself wholeheartedly to this great subject. The conception just described is an abstraction from the play. Danton belongs to it, but not all of Danton. In this part Büchner uses Danton to focus disillusion and his own insight, gained from grievous experience, into the tangle of all human action, in which the forces outside men are seen as the decisive and true agents of events. But there is a more disturbing Danton than this symbolic figure. In the historical Danton the feature of paralysis of will, setting in somewhat unaccountably, was noted by the historians whom Büchner studied as his sources, and was taken over by him as an important motive in the action, such as it is, of his play. But this historical Danton's sudden weariness, his not wanting to go on shedding blood, not wanting to become simply a tyrant, is something very different from loathing and disgust with life, from reckless cynicism, from the denial of all ideals, meaning and value, and from the morbid reduction of things human and suprahuman to senseless corruption. This Danton —the Danton of *Langeweile*, of the nihilistic world-chaos, the Danton who identifies the sensation of love with that of the grave, who seeks macabre images or exaggerative and defiantly cynical epitomizations to describe life—this is, in my view, not the same Danton, developed and made fuller and richer, but a different one, added to the play, and related to the other only as a caricature. This is Georg Büchner's private Danton. The language he speaks, the attitude he embodies, are not insincere, but they spoil the play. They bring in a pessimism of a lurid, brutish, and sordid kind, making the work in some parts simply ugly and tedious.

No one, to my knowledge, has thus ventured to see two Dantons in Büchner's play. It is, however, on this very point of Danton's *extreme* pessimism, that interpretations actually fall apart. This is where the play, for those who oppose the sociological view, offers decisive evidence of having a "metaphysical" foundation, or a universalized human tragic note, or a "religious" meaning, or of being a nihilistic gospel. I do not agree with these interpretations. They arise from the assumption, all too common, that poetic works express *a priori* a valid, finalized *Weltanschauung*, or perhaps also from the habit of taking scattered statements too absolutely and constructing from them logical and systematic schemes of thought. I do agree, however, that the feature of Danton's character under consideration makes the play less of a sociopolitical one; but it also, in my view, makes it a worse play, not a "deeper," or more "tragic," or more "religious" one. I prefer to see here a disunity in the play that is a symptom both of Büchner's philosophical and of his poetic-dramatic immaturity.

His immaturity caused him to miss an opportunity; with greater and cooler mastery of architectonic form and of the development of dramatic scenes (he is rudimentary in this respect), with a greater sense of dramatic *art* supplementing his natural sense of dramatic event, he could have developed to perfection the noble play that never really bursts out of the shadows thrown by the sickening *Weltschmerz* of Danton. Lukács, with a sympathy proceeding from his political interests, spotted this; but he sees only the noble play and not the sordid one. In the former, Danton is still a heroic figure, in the latter only a mouthpiece for Büchner reviling man and nature in a phase of sullen desperation, which is not heroic at all. Danton's emotional outbursts in this mood are crude and unsightly; to glorify them as the profound expression of a cosmic despair is to lose the sense of the genuine poetic. It is common to suggest a kinship in Büchner with the *Geniezeit*, especially since the word *Genie* is felt to sum up his mental complexion in a quite special way. But the naked emotionalism, the frank violence of rebellious passions, the emphatic defiance, of the *Sturm und Drang*, distasteful as they are to a refined taste, rested on an ideal of nature and human fulfilment, and they were, however extravagant, a courageous protest against effete rationalism and stifling social conventions. Danton's "protest" is by comparison morbid and decadent. Similarly, the comparison with the great philosophical pessimists and rebels breaks down. At the side of Schopenhauer, or Kierkegaard, or Nietzsche, Büchner's ideas are elementary and his emotional reactions those of a layman.

Woyzeck is a different matter. The reason seems to me simple; the gall has been forgotten and charity has taken its place, so that tragedy is achieved without a jarring note. The intense tragic effect, to which all respond, however they seek to explain it, derives from the presence of human compassion which only a faith makes possible. In *Dantons Tod* the potential tragedy of revolution is drowned in the negative unbelief of the ugly Danton; nihilism, even if it is only theoretical and verbal, excludes tragedy. In *Woyzeck* we have a great and moving compassion for a human being, and a vigorous and noble implicit protest against social failure.

This play, fragment though it is, has a unity absent in *Dantons Tod*, a unity, moreover, that embraces both the social and the general human sentiment. In fact, they cannot here be separated, and, far from being in conflict, reinforce each other. Woyzeck is a simple man of the people, living in poverty and ignorance, without any vestige, or chance, of civilized living, a man dominated by the most elementary needs and feelings of nature, the tool of his superiors, physically unequal to his rival, helpless in his love and suffering. He represents vividly man in a condition of social deprivation. By nature man is only partly brutish; he is more so when kept poor and in servitude. When Woyzeck murders it is partly a failure in the nature of man, if he remains animal and savage, but partly a failure in society, when it fails to do what it can to humanize its own members. Yet Woyzeck is not simply a brute—what sympathy should we have for him otherwise?—but a human being with a loyal love and at least a remnant of pride. He is human because he loves and is faithful, because he aspires in his mute way to something higher, and because he is sinned against. This situation, however commonplace, is always tragic, and Büchner has presented it with a beautiful spareness and simplicity that make it moving. But it is rendered more interesting and enormously strengthened by the social implications. Woyzeck is persecuted by a society divided into haves and have-nots. His helplessness, and the pity it evokes, are at once social and human.

Many are unwilling to accept this view, because they feel that Woyzeck is a symbol of man's general solitude and stricken condition. He is not an interesting or complex enough character, however, to be such a representative. A valid spiritual despair, a genuine human accusation against God or the universe, can only be presented with the subtlest arguments of the soul, and never with the stammerings of the inarticulate. Moreover, apart from this general argument, it is entirely reasonable, in view of Büchner's political opinions and activities in Hesse, to give Woyzeck a social meaning. It makes better sense, too. Especially one understands more easily the harsh or patronizing parts played by the Doctor and the Captain, or such things as the introduction of the satirical scene about animal and social behavior at the fairground, or the comment of the Polizist at the end: "Ein guter Mord, ein echter Mord, ein schöner Mord." The representative of the public order recognizes, from his superior bourgeois point of view, a crime that goes neatly into his categories, a perfect specimen of what one expects from the "criminal classes." Pity for the human condition, for the misery of life, is particularized here in relation to one of its forms, the social one. And because Büchner manages to express this without falling in any way into doctrinaire statements the play shows human and social tragedy conjoined. With his gaze on both man and society steadier, with his social philosophy unobtrusive but firm, Büchner's picture of tragedy is more convincing, more charitable, and more moving. In its unity of vision and effect appears the greater maturity of *Woyzeck,* as compared with *Dantons Tod,* both in its philosophical tone and in its dramatic expression.

Just as the interpretation of Büchner's meanings tends to emphasize either a social vision or a tragic disillusion so also the interpretation of his style pendulates between the appreciation of a strong "realism" and a poetic expression of "Stimmungen." And again, it seems to me, the error is to see these as mutually exclusive.

With regard to realism, there is a tendency for this term, used of Büchner, sometimes to mean the political thinker and sometimes to refer to his dramatic style. On the former score he was undoubtedly a realist by comparison with the political "liberals" whose reformist zeal was sentimentally humane and idealistic. He has the distinction of being unusually aware for his time of the economic motive in society. His Hessian insurrectionism was directed against the "rich," not merely against the feudal ruling class. He was one of the first to adopt an essentially two-level class analysis, anticipating a much later development.

How much has this to do with realism in his style? Something, but not everything. It accounts for the choice of Woyzeck as a subject; for the "poor wretch" as hero and for the adoption of a true criminal case as his documentary foundation. It was a new realism of subject, showing Büchner taking a very decisive step beyond the classic-romantic era. A realist intention also informs his treatment of history in *Dantons Tod*. He subscribed to the view that the dramatist should be perfectly faithful to historical fact. Although it can be argued that he did in fact exercise choice in using his sources, he seems to have done so only within narrow limits. He certainly did not alter facts, and he quite deliberately avoided idealization in the manner of Schiller or in the interests of a "universal" idea. The scenes with populace in both *Dantons Tod* and *Woyzeck* show his realism as a matter of sincerity and of taste.

The same anti-idealistic spirit informs his much-quoted remarks in *Lenz* about simple truth to nature as the proper ideal for poets; the vitality of the created thing, its living quality, is the true criterion, and it doesn't matter whether it is beautiful or ugly. It is rare to find it, moreover; it meets us in Shakespeare, in folk poetry, sometimes in Goethe. In this famous passage, however, there are some remarks that are not usually quoted but are in my view crucial for the understanding of Büchner's ideal of style. "Dieser Idealismus ist die schmählichste Verachtung der menschlichen Natur. Man versuche es einmal und senke sich in das Leben des Geringsten und gebe es wieder in den Zuckungen, den Andeutungen, dem ganzen feinen, kaum bemerkten Mienenspiel; er [i.e. Lenz] hätte dergleichen versucht im 'Hofmeister' und den 'Soldaten.' Es sind die prosaischsten Menschen unter der Sonne; aber die Gefühlsader ist in fast allen Menschen gleich, nur ist die Hülle mehr oder weniger dicht, durch die sie brechen muss. Man muss nur Aug und Ohren dafür haben. Wie ich gestern neben am Tal hinaufging, sah ich auf einem Steine zwei Mädchen sitzen: die eine band ihre Haare auf, die andre half ihr; und das goldne Haar hing herab, und ein ernstes bleiches Gesicht, und doch so jung, und die schwarze Tracht, und die andre so sorgsam bemüht. Die schönsten, innigsten Bilder der altdeutschen Schule geben kaum eine Ahnung davon." The ideal suggested here departs from realistic presentation proper and instead places the universals of *feeling* in the center; it selects its pictures according to their manner of evoking responsive emotions. This is of great significance because it corresponds to what actually occurs in Büchner's execution of his dramatic scenes. It gives the clue to the rare quality in these scenes which makes them so poetically moving and raises them above the element of squalid truth that their realistic setting comprehends. This brings me back to what I said was one of the dominant impressions received from Büchner's work.

Büchner handles material that is fraught with drama, without following the convention—a good one, let us remind ourselves, though German critics underestimate its value, accepting too easily dramatic turbulence for dramatic art—of making a good plot. There is no plot, or only very little, in *Dantons Tod.* Danton and his friends are in danger, they are arrested, they wait in dejection for their fate to be decided, and finally they are taken to the guillotine. There is no real dramatic development within the separate scenes; Büchner is almost innocent of the interlocking clash of purposes which is the working material of the dramatist. The basic conflict scarcely appears in the dialectic of scene and dialogue, but only from virtually monolithic statements on either side at different times, and even the one short scene between Danton and Robespierre is fundamentally similar—an opposition of statements rather than a passionate grappling of two wills and their actions. There are, moreover, too many characters, too many incidental persons without a sustained role, for dramatic clarity. Frequent change of scene suggests movement, yet the essential rhythm of a dramatic concatenation is missing. *Woyzeck* also has little plot. It is in effect a chronicle, a narrative sequence of scenes, given tension, however, by the simple jealousy story working up to the climax of murder.

But what is really original in Büchner is his mastery in framing the pregnant emotional or dramatic instant. These instants have a character quite their own. They are anything but "short dramatic scenes" of vivid action or genre portraiture. In the latter category I would put, for example, the "Bude" scene in *Woyzeck*, or the scene "Eine Gasse" (Simon and his wife) in *Dantons Tod*, Act I. They are good scenes, but Büchner becomes really remarkable with the kind that have for their purpose the focusing of intense phases of feeling and mood. At their best such scenes have a dramatic reference; they are the high points of a story, arranged in narrative sequence but with selective and concentrated dramatic significance. Two of the "Mariens Kammer" scenes in *Woyzeck* are good examples. The first is where Marie has received gifts from her new lover, and Woyzeck finds her with them and gets his first fleeting suspicions. There is no attempt to develop a violent scene between them, to elaborate a conflict. On the contrary there is an agreement of feeling in the sense of poverty they both have, and the end of the short episode, its climax, is Marie's remorseful feeling of wickedness followed by the indifference of despair. The second example shows another pregnant moment when the light is focused for an instant on a phase of emotion. Marie is here with her bastard child and the Narr, a grotesque partner in the scene. She is driven to her Bible by the consciousness of her sin and faithlessness. She reads phrases about the woman taken in adultery and intersperses exclamations of remorse; the Narr repeats nonsensical bits from fairy stories and then is silent, holding the child. Wholly unconventional in technique, the dramatic significance of this scene lies in its presenting the moment of moral breakdown in Marie. The presence of the idiot gives something additional to the psychological drama, enlarging the scene to make it reflect a greater discordance in life.

Büchner packs his dramatic excitements into scenes of this kind. But they do have a curiously ambiguous quality. It is no doubt a dramatic interest that isolates such highly charged instants, but they can sometimes have an effect more lyrical than dramatic; though it must also be added that the quality is not adequately described by the term "Stimmung." The scene of the murder in *Woyzeck*, for example, set with a maximum of "atmosphere"—the forest, the pond, the cold night air, the blood-red moon—is given, beyond its meaning as action or climax of the story, the quality of a nightmare. It only comes to an end in a violent act; in itself it shows action suspended in Woyzeck's brooding and Marie's passive unknowingness. Often there is no action at all, or a minimum. The actual substance of many of Büchner's scenes is the pointed crystallization of emotion or mood in one of the principal persons, making a self-sufficient picture, by contrast with the more usual construction in which the crisscrossed lines of plot and action flow through every scene. His most beautiful and poetic moments are of this kind. One thinks of Danton and Julie in Act II, of the Lucile scenes at the end of the same play, of Julie taking poison, or of the great sadness of the Conciergerie scene in Act IV. Such scenes emerge, it is true enough, from a story or dramatic framework, but their nature is to be brief acted lyrics. Their predominant themes, moreover, are love, a wistful sense of nature and its moods, and the helplessness, solitude, and terror of men.

In this, Büchner's strongest poetic vein, he was very much a late romantic. There is no need to feel that this contradicts his politics or such realism as he has or that it reduces his status. His politics, like most progressive movements of the nineteenth century, derive ultimately from Rousseau's idealism, which was a political aspect of the romanticism that spread through Europe in the later eighteenth century and found varying literary expression as well. Democratic faiths and romantic moods went very well together in many writers of the eighteen-twenties and thirties. Büchner's moods of despair, cynicism, boredom, his motifs of death and corruption, his meaningless universe, his fatalism, his ear for a beautiful but also a sinister music in nature and the empty spaces, his glimpses into hallucination, nightmare, and madness, all these are the common stock of much romantic literature. His conception of realism in art, meaning the simple natural truth of things and men, is also after all tinged with romanticism, just as poeticization by the use of *Volkslieder* is a romantic, not a realist, symptom. His hard-boiled political attitude, the atheism, the sober, unadorned scientific materialism, indicate perhaps an unromantic attitude that was to be possible in the future; in Büchner they are still a result of emotional reaction, not an entirely new, free beginning. From such attitudes there arose later in the century a characteristic realist style in literature. Büchner belongs to the period in which realist insights still jostled with romantic longings and above all with romantic poetic ideals. Even with a changing subject matter the expression continued to reflect the romantic style. It is a mistake to be prejudiced one way or the other in Büchner's case, and see only half the picture. His finest scenes owe their character, their beauty, and their own original, rare quality to a romantic lyricism that flowers amidst intimations of a new, socially realistic subject.

INDEX

DRAMABOOKS

Hill and Wang has established DRAMABOOKS as a permanent library of the great classics of the theatre of all countries, in an attractive, low-priced format.

Plays

MD 1 *Christopher Marlowe* edited by Havelock Ellis. Introduction by John Addington Symonds (Tamburlaine the Great, Parts I & II, Doctor Faustus, The Jew of Malta, Edward the Second)

MD 2 *William Congreve* edited by Alexander Charles Ewald. Introduction by Macaulay (Complete Plays)

MD 3 *Webster and Tourneur* Introduction by John Addington Symonds (The White Devil, The Duchess of Malfi, The Atheist's Tragedy, The Revenger's Tragedy)

MD 4 *John Ford* edited by Havelock Ellis (The Lover's Melancholy, 'Tis Pity She's a Whore, The Broken Heart, Love's Sacrifice, Perkin Warbeck)

MD 5 *Richard Brinsley Sheridan* edited with an Introduction by Louis Kronenberger (The Rivals, St. Patrick's Day, The Duenna, A Trip to Scarborough, The School for Scandal, The Critic)

MD 6 *Camille and Other Plays* edited, with an Introduction to the well-made play by Stephen S. Stanton (Scribe: A Peculiar Position, and The Glass of Water; Sardou: A Scrap of Paper; Dumas, *fils*: Camille; Augier: Olympe's Marriage)

MD 7 *John Dryden* edited, and with an Introduction by George Saintsbury (The Conquest of Granada, Parts I & II, Marriage à la Mode, Aureng-Zebe)

MD 8 *Ben Jonson* edited, with an Introduction and Notes, by Brinsley Nicholson and C. H. Herford (Volpone, Epicoene, The Alchemist)

MD 9 *Oliver Goldsmith* edited by George Pierce Baker with an Introduction by Austin Dobson (The Good Natur'd Man, She Stoops to Conquer, An Essay on the Theatre, A Register of Scotch Marriages)

MD 10 *Jean Anouilh* Volume 1 (Antigone, Eurydice, The Rehearsal, Romeo and Jeannette, The Ermine)

MD 11 *Let's Get a Divorce! and Other Plays,* edited, and with an Introduction on The Psychology of Farce by Eric Bentley (Labiche: A Trip Abroad, and Célimare; Sardou: Let's Get a Divorce!; Courteline, These Cornfields; Feydeau: Keep an Eye on Amélie; Prévert: A United Family; Achard: essay on Feydeau)

MD 12 *Jean Giraudoux* adapted and with an Introduction by Maurice Valency (Ondine, The Enchanted, The Madwoman of Chaillot, The Apollo of Bellac)

MD 13 *Jean Anouilh* Volume 2 (Restless Heart, Time Remembered, Ardèle, Mademoiselle Colombe, The Lark)

MD 14 *Henrik Ibsen: The Last Plays* Introduction and translation by William Archer (Little Eyolf, John Gabriel Borkman, When We Dead Awaken)

MD 15 *Ivan Turgenev* translated by Constance Garnett (A Month in the Country, A Provincial Lady, A Poor Gentleman)

Plays (*continued*)

MD 16 *George Farquhar* edited, with an Introduction and Notes, by William Archer (The Constant Couple, The Twin-Rivals, The Recruiting Officer, The Beaux' Stratagem)
MD 17 *Jean Racine: Five Plays* Introduction and translation by Kenneth Muir (Andromache, Britannicus, Berenice, Phaedra, Athaliah)
MD 18 *The Storm and Other Russian Plays* Introduction and translation by David Magarshack (The Storm, The Government Inspector, The Power of Darkness, Uncle Vanya, The Lower Depths)
MD 19 *Michel de Ghelderode* Introduction by George Hauger (The Ostend Interviews, Chronicles of Hell, Barabbas, The Women at the Tomb, Pantagleize, The Blind Men, Three Players and a Play, Lord Halewyn)
SD 1 *The Last Days of Lincoln* by Mark Van Doren
SD 2 *Oh Dad, Poor Dad, Mamma's Hung You in the Closet and I'm Feelin' So Sad* by Arthur L. Kopit

Criticism

D 1 *Shakespeare and the Elizabethans* by Henri Fluchère. Foreword by T. S. Eliot
D 2 *On Dramatic Method* by Harley Granville-Barker
D 3 *George Bernard Shaw* by G. K. Chesterton
D 4 *The Paradox of Acting* by Denis Diderot and *Masks or Faces?* by William Archer. Introduction by Lee Strasberg
D 5 *The Scenic Art* by Henry James. Edited with an Introduction and Notes by Allan Wade
D 6 *Preface to Hamlet* by Harley Granville-Barker
D 7 *Hazlitt on Theatre* edited by William Archer and Robert Lowe. Introduction by William Archer
D 8 *The Fervent Years* by Harold Clurman
D 9 *The Quintessence of Ibsenism* by Bernard Shaw
D 10 *Papers on Playmaking* edited by Brander Matthews
D 11 *Papers on Acting* edited by Brander Matthews
D 12 *The Theatre* by Stark Young
D 13 *Immortal Shadows* by Stark Young
D 14 *Shakespeare: A Survey* by E. K. Chambers
D 15 *The English Dramatic Critics* edited by James Agate
D 16 *Japanese Theatre* by Faubion Bowers
D 17 *Shaw's Dramatic Criticism* (1895-98) edited by John F. Matthews
D 18 *Shaw on Theatre* edited by E. J. West
D 19 *The Book of Job as a Greek Tragedy* by Horace Meyer Kallen
D 20 *Molière: The Man Seen Through the Plays* by Ramon Fernandez. Translation by Wilson Follett
D 21 *Greek Tragedy* by Gilbert Norwood
D 22 *Samuel Johnson on Shakespeare* edited with an Introduction by W. K. Wimsatt, Jr.
D 23 *The Poet in the Theatre* by Ronald Peacock
D 24 *Chekhov the Dramatist* by David Magarshack
D 25 *Theory and Technique of Playwriting* by John Howard Lawson